Violins & Spoons

Cover by Jay Thompson, inspired from an original painting by Paul Squires

Editing, design, typesetting and publishing by UK Book Publishing

www.ukbookpublishing.com

ISBN: 978-1-918077-47-6

Violins & Spoons

Catherine Atkinson

UK BookPublishing.com

Foreword

—

Having had a career as a children's doctor specialising in cancer and also having held national and international roles with a variety of organisations related to paediatrics and the well-being of children I can recommend this book to a wide audience of people. For some it may be that their lives have been impacted by children's cancer; for others it may be the dilemmas and conflicts which they have experienced as a result of adoption; whilst others may find inspiration in Catherine's dogged determination to navigate paternalistic attitudes in the health service and subsequently, and over many years, to navigate state bureaucracy in both England and Canada.

Catherine had a happy childhood and enjoyed a successful career, first as a nurse, then as an academic within the field of textile design, before managing properties for the National Trust, including Lindisfarne Castle on Holy Island in Northumberland. She is very happily married to her soul-mate Peter, a proud mother to three children and now a grandmother. Her need to trace her birth parents was something which developed slowly, but once fully recognised she allowed no stone to go unturned regardless of the many barriers put in her way over many years. Her story has a recurring theme of loss as it affected in very different ways herself, her birth mother and her adoptive mother.

Many of you will have watched '*Who do you think you are*', which can be fascinating, but when the subject is someone you know and admire it has more meaning. I have known Catherine for several decades as she and my wife started their nursing careers together, I had some inkling of her back story, and this book tells of the many challenges Catherine has encountered in her journey to find out who she was, to connect with her roots, and to take comfort in finding some traits common to both her birth and adoptive parents; and perhaps even more importantly provide her children with an understanding of their heritage, something which was denied to her for almost half a century.

Professor Sir Alan Craft
Emeritus Professor of Child Health
Former President of the Royal College of Paediatrics and Children
Former Chairman of the UK Scout Association

Preface

My motivation for sharing my story about adoption and my son's illness was simply a need to put it in writing. I appreciate the support from my children, family, and friends, especially my husband Peter, and Pat and Jennifer from Durham. Some names have been changed.

Catherine Atkinson

Contents

___

PART 4: CONCEALMENT AND PERSISTENCE

PART 5: SHED THE GUILT AND BURY THE BLAME

Part 1:

—

Early Years and Realisation

Chapter 1

At the age of 38 I hadn't expected to find myself emotionally lost and adrift with no firm anchor to my life. It was October 1983, the day of my father's memorial service in Durham Cathedral. I arrived at the Cathedral, from Wakefield, with my husband, Peter, and our three young children. Reservations had been made in the choir stalls for close relatives. When we approached the choir, the verger told us we would have to sit somewhere in the nave as all the stalls in the choir were taken. That was strange as my father didn't have many close relatives, only his brother and sister and my brother. I did explain that it was my father's memorial service and these were his grandchildren. But this made no impression on the busy verger who was trying to sort out the considerable number of people who were filling the Cathedral. The Cathedral had been my father's life. He had first been a choirboy in 1913, at the age of nine, and then progressed to becoming an ordained priest.

In 1983 both my parents died within months of each other, my father aged 79 and my mother 72. It was a sad year, as my mother died from cancer and my father had Alzheimer's. They had been my parents since I was under a year old, and I loved them dearly. Now I was close to tears. My father had spent almost sixty years attached to the Cathedral. I wanted to sit in the choir and have his memory close to me. I remembered my father as a studious, balding and slightly built person. He hadn't been someone to seek favours or privileges. Neither had he been an ambitious person. Nor did he enjoy being the focus of attention. Without hesitation, he would have sat quietly where he was directed. His voice was saying to me, "Just sit where you are told", so we sat obligingly in the nave amongst the rest of the congregation. After all, it was the service that was important, not the seating arrangements. The occasion belonged to my father and not to me. But I couldn't help feeling isolated and abandoned, even though I was with my husband and children. I imagined that everyone in the Cathedral was staring at me, thinking you are not his biological daughter, so you have no right to have a privileged seat in the choir. Yet he had been my father for nearly forty years, and this was the place where I grew up.

I was unable to concentrate on the service. I couldn't stop my mind drifting towards my childhood. In 1955, two years before I went to an all-girls boarding school, I discovered that I was adopted. However, at the age of ten, I found the idea exciting. Up until this point, I had no indication that I was not the child of my parents. At my primary school, we mused with each other about being adopted. It sounded romantic and the basis of fairy tales. I had heard the terms bastard, illegitimate and "being born on the wrong side of the blanket", but I never thought any of it referred to me. I understood little of the meaning of these words but was captivated by the idea of adoption.

The large, ten-foot-long, kitchen table, in my childhood home next to the Cathedral, was the place for all discussions. The kitchen was a warm, friendly room with a range cooker being the main source of heat. It was open house for anyone to pop in for a chat and to have a cup of tea. On the day of the school playground adoption chat, I arrived home from school to find my mother in the kitchen standing by the cooker. I asked her the straightforward question, "Am I adopted?" And my mother replied, "Yes," as directly as I had asked. I was elated. I could go back to school and tell my classmates, "Actually, I was adopted." I felt like a celebrity. The social implications of being adopted certainly didn't occur to me at that point. After much pestering, my mother was only prepared to say that she had specially chosen me. I was so naive I didn't have any idea about childbirth. I knew that animals gave birth to their young, but I was not sure about humans.

At school one of the teachers heard me boasting to my friends about being adopted. She took me to one side and told me I must never talk about the subject to anyone, or my parents would be angry. I was confused. How was this? I had been told by my mother that I had been specifically chosen over other babies. I could not understand the reasoning behind what this teacher was telling me. I was deflated and bewildered, and my confidence vanished. After this, I left the subject alone and asked no more questions.

Following the teacher's comment, I was aware that adoption was not a subject that should be openly discussed. I didn't probe my mother again about my adoption until I was fifteen. By this time, I was more aware of how women became pregnant. I was home from boarding school as it was the Easter holidays, and I started to push my mother for further details of my birth. She was reluctant to tell me much. I believed the little she did tell me was all she knew. She said she went to a baby's home and specifically asked for a white baby with fair hair and blue eyes, which of course I have. I guessed that if my mother adopted a child with similar looks to herself, she could pretend to the world that she had conceived me. It was strange how people would often comment on how alike we were.

I'm not sure how this could be, especially when she had size three feet, and I have the enormous size nine. I have a slim, long face and hers was round and pretty.

My mother told me my parents were Canadian, my name had been Donna Mary Hamilton and in 1945 I was born in Petersfield Hospital in Hampshire. It shocked me that my name had been changed. It never occurred to me this would have happened. Was my whole identity a lie? I went back to boarding school with a sense of not knowing who I was. I knew my friends so well at school, but now, did they know me? I was a fraud. I did try to tell one friend that my real name was Donna Mary, when she knew me as Catherine. She thought I was making it up or being a drama queen. The truth of the matter was that she was not interested. I became nervous and embarrassed to ever raise the subject again until much later in my life.

My father's memorial service intensified the feeling of being rootless with no past. Sitting on the hard upright pews in the nave of the Cathedral, all I could think about was, that I was adopted, I didn't belong, and I had no blood entitlement. My mind was full of self-doubts. But why should this be, when my mother and father had been like any other parents who made sacrifices for their children? They had given me a loving, privileged home, a little odd at times, but I didn't doubt that my parents had deep affection for me. Their deaths left me perplexed with a sense of displacement.

The Cathedral's colossal sandstone structure was reassuring; it had been an enduring anchor to my life. I saw the Cathedral as my home just as much as the nearby house where I grew up. During my father's memorial service my mind wandered. I needed to remind myself that I had a place in the world and that place was here in this building. But the question of "who am I?" seemed stronger than ever. Why was it so important for me to know my genetic origins? I thought about this and concluded that I was grieving for my parents and suffering from emotional self-indulgence and self-pity, which I decided was not an attractive trait. Nevertheless, as hard as I tried not to reflect on these thoughts, they were stuck in my mind. I was trying to make sense of the melancholy I was feeling. I was in limbo and was desperately in need of a solid past. Now my parents were dead, I had no right to belong to their family history. It was as if I had been given to them on loan. I was borrowing an identity that was now gone. I was confused and displaced. This was compounded by the fact that, as a teenager, my maternal grandmother had told me I could not be added to her family tree as I was not a blood relative. The one thing that was of comfort, was the fabric of the Cathedral, every nuance of which was so familiar.

My father had taken services at the Cathedral since I was a small child. He had devoted his life to the Cathedral until his retirement in 1972. His remains are interred in the grounds under the sculptured panel depicting the milkmaids and a Dun Cow. This is high up on the wall at the northeast side of the Cathedral. A plaque, in memory of his time at the Cathedral, was placed at the entrance to the Song School. The Song School is where the teaching and practice of ecclesiastical music and singing takes place.

During the memorial service, I gazed high up into the ribbed stone vaulted lantern of the Cathedral tower. The lantern, some hundred feet above the crossing, has a walkway around it with a waist-high stone balustrade. The loft above the ceiling of the lantern is the bell ringers' chamber which is just below the belfry that houses the Cathedral's ten bells. The familiarity of the stonework and the belfry gave me a sense of peace and security, reminding me of my youth. I knew every inch of the Cathedral – as a young girl it had been my adventure playground.

My parents married in 1932 but did not adopt my elder brother until 1943. I followed in 1946 at the age of six months. There was a sadness about my mother as she desperately wanted to give birth to her own offspring. It must have been a difficult burden to bear. When I was a mature woman, my mother told me she had married my father at the age of twenty-one. Shortly after the wedding, she became ill and nearly died in hospital from a secondary infection following a bout of scarlet fever. This would have been profoundly serious and life-threatening in the early 1930s before penicillin was widely available. Following this illness, she was diagnosed with a cyst on one of her ovaries. She returned to hospital for an operation to remove the offending ovary. The surgeon decided to whip out the other ovary for good measure. I can't imagine that happening today in the twenty-first century. I know my mother suffered greatly both physically and emotionally after her operation. Her infertility left a deep void in her life. Would my adopted brother and I ever have been able to fill the gap?

Both my parents were good musicians, especially my mother, who was a gifted professional violinist. Her violin was her passion in life. She was also an accomplished pianist. Before my mother married, she studied the violin at the Royal Academy of Music in London and won many awards. She also played for the BBC. Now, decades after her death, I realise that I have no photographs of her playing her violin. All these years later this seems quite sad as my most endearing memory of her is with a violin under her chin.

From an early age, my mother had known that she would be a professional musician. My grandmother did not send her to school but tutored her at home in all academic subjects including Latin and mathematics. These lessons fitted in around her music practice. At the age of eight, she was practising her violin six to eight hours a day. This is what made her a shy person and emotionally distant. The love of classical music was the one thing my parents had in common. My father played the organ and piano, and they performed in local orchestras. My mother being the lead violinist while my father would switch from piano to being a drummer and percussionist. From a young age I would sit by the edge of the orchestra pit to watch and listen to the music. These performances were mostly popular operas by Mozart or Gilbert and Sullivan. My father liked Gilbert and Sullivan. However, my mother was not a fan of light opera. There appeared to be no intimacy between my parents. I wondered if my mother would have married if she had she known she could not conceive children. Would she have dedicated her life to her violin instead?

As an eight-year-old, I had tried the violin but failed to get further than Twinkle Twinkle Little Star. Why had my mother not recognised that my aptitude for music was not likely to develop? Why had she not said anything? But wanting to please my mother, and having the necessary large hands, I asked to learn the piano while I was away at boarding school.

My tutor was an elderly woman, of fifty or sixty. I must admit I found it difficult to assess the age of someone over about thirty-five as they all looked old. So my tutor may have only been forty. She was as wide as she was tall, with skin-coloured thick stockings that wrinkled round her ankles. She wore a dreary, heavyweight tweed skirt with a "bosomy" blouse and no makeup. I was never going to succeed because when I looked at the notes laid out on the music sheet, all I could see were patterns, not musical notes. One of the shapes was the sign "Ped". This showed that I should press down the right-hand piano foot pedal. To me, "Ped" looked like little elephants walking around underneath the music bars, which amused me and made me lose my place on the page.

In the middle of one piano lesson, I heard my teacher shout, "No, no, no. Why can't you play like your mother?" Then the grand piano lid came slamming down on my hands. "I can't teach you anymore, just leave." Near to tears, I left the room without saying a word. I could not think of what I was supposed to do. The tears were not because my hands hurt. Due to my fast reaction, the lid hardly caught the tips of my fingers. It was because of my musical ability. I was despondent. I was not sure how I was going to explain to my mother that I had been thrown out of my piano lesson.

At school, in my teenage years, I never gave up trying to be musical. After the piano, I attempted the recorder, then the flute, and the choir. I was disappointed in myself as I had failed my musical parents. I can't put my failure down to any bad teaching at school but my lack of dedication, as I preferred to read a book than work on my music practice. Now, at my father's memorial service, listening to the Cathedral choir singing, I know I should have tried harder to make my mother proud of her daughter. It did not help that my music teachers knew of my mother's talent. What they did not know was that we did not have the same genetic makeup. Talking of not giving up, recently I have been for singing lessons, but I'm not sure where that will lead. Painful for everyone else I suspect.

We were not what you might imagine to be the typical clergyman's family. Apart from her violin, my mother bred Siamese cats and had a small farm half a mile from the house. She rented a few acres of land from the Dean and Chapter, and kept goats, pigs, hens, and a few geese. Early on Sunday mornings, as every day, she would get into her Wellington boots and head to the farm. She was a neat, trim, attractive person, who liked expensive clothes. However, following the example of the wives of other clergymen by looking smart on Sundays was not for her. She rarely conformed and was a breath of fresh air within the pretentious environment of the Cathedral College, sometimes called a Cathedral Close. She allowed my brother and me the freedom to develop our personalities, more than likely to the consternation of my father. He held the Victorian concept that children should be seen and not heard. He was occupied most of the time in the Cathedral or teaching at the Chorister School. Apart from the Cathedral, my other playground was my mother's farm where I sat for hours up trees as well as learning to milk the goats.

My mother was fiercely independent and bought me up to be the same. She was immensely practical as well as academically bright. Everything she did was to perfection. I would have loved to have had her attributes. But what of my birth mother? She is someone I knew nothing about, not even a photograph. Does she have a sadness about her life having to give me up at birth?

Leaving the Cathedral, after the memorial service, to travel the hundred miles south home to Wakefield, was like leaving my childhood behind. I was forced to face up to the enormity of my adoption. Losing two mothers, one at birth and the other when I was aged thirty-eight was a difficult concept and baffling to work out where my disconnection lay. Did it stem from when I was separated from my birth mother, or was it that my parents were now both dead? After all, it was normal to feel sad at my father's memorial service. I was saying goodbye to both my parents, my mother as well as my father. What I didn't know, sitting in the Cathedral listening to my father's service, was that in just a few years, as a family we would suffer immeasurable grief and sadness.

Chapter 2

After the age of fifteen and up to when my parents died in 1983, I had only fleeting thoughts about being adopted. When I was away at boarding school, I never wanted to raise the subject. Partly because I hated being away at school and partly because I was poor at expressing my feelings. If I couldn't explain my emotions to myself, how could I describe how I felt to others?

At my boarding school, the worst thing was the lack of privacy, the draconian rules, and strict controls in place. The institution was boring and mundane with pointless regulations. It was miserable both emotionally and physically. But most of all I hated the feeling of homelessness and the lack of freedom. The headmistress must have read the Rules of Saint Benedict, written for monks in the sixth century. Chapter five prescribes prompt, ungrudging and absolute blind obedience to your superior. It was obvious that my headmistress was obsessed with "unhesitating obedience", as was St Benedict. It was't for me. I was not a good student and was always looking for ways to question these oppressive rules.

When I was sixteen, at the end of the fifth form, I was asked to leave. This suited me fine. I could not have been happier. I persuaded my parents that going to the local Durham Technical College would be a much better way forward for my education. Once home, at the end of term, I managed to intercept a letter from the headmistress. My parents never realised I had been thrown out of school.

In 1963, I went into nursing, which was something I had wanted to do since being a small child. There was the odd diversion when I thought I would be a police officer or a nun. Ballet dancing and being an opera singer were also on my agenda, but my lack of musical ability soon quashed those ideas. I also dreamt of being an astronaut and wanted to be the first woman in space. I suffer from travel sickness so perhaps a space trip would not have been a clever plan. These thoughts were short-lived anyway, and I always returned to the idea of being a nurse.

I entered the nurses' training school at the Royal Victoria Infirmary (RVI) in Newcastle two days before my eighteenth birthday. The training lasted three years, after which I gained my State Registered Nursing qualification (SRN). The tuition consisted of practical work and "on-the-job" learning, interspersed with periods in the classroom. I had twelve weeks initially in class before being let loose on the wards.

During the first few weeks of my training, we had a lecture by a representative from a company that made sanitary products. This visiting lecturer was an ex-nurse, and her job now was to teach us about the anatomy of human reproduction. After all, in those days of school education, there might be a confused talk about how rabbits produced lots of babies by just looking at each other. That was certainly my experience at boarding school. In 1963, the subject was too embarrassing for our regular spinster nursing tutors to tackle. But true to the curriculum, the straight-talking visiting tutor duly explained, in detail, all she thought we needed to know. She finished by saying that male medical students were evil as they only wanted to pinch our bottoms and get into our knickers. The class, by this point, had all switched off and had stopped listening. I was innocent, having been to my all-girls boarding school, so I hung on her every word. I was the only girl in the class who had been away at school. It was more than likely that my birth mother would have been a single woman and that is why she gave me up for adoption. I paid attention to the warning about medical students as I did not want history to repeat itself.

Contraception was a bit of a hit-and-miss affair back in the 1960s. Warnings about unplanned pregnancies were well-meaning. I had the resolve not to get pregnant before I was married. Once, when my mother picked up that I was "partying" she came out with the cruel remark of, "…well, like mother, like daughter". I don't think she meant to be hurtful, it was just her way of saying beware of what can happen. At that moment I knew I could never go home pregnant out of wedlock. I guessed also that my birth mother felt she could not go home with a new baby in her arms and no husband.

After qualifying it was expected that I would complete an additional post-graduation year. Matron thought our education was not complete without the extra year. Or was it a ploy to make sure her hospital was well-staffed with staff nurses trained in her likeness to run the wards? This was years before nurses became university graduates and directors of nursing. There were no television consoles for each bed or disposable bedpans. Resistant superbugs had hardly been heard of and there were few disposable items. Like today, however, there were bed shortages, waiting lists, infection concerns and recruitment issues.

Also, there were incidents of nurses being attacked by patients. One night, as a student nurse, I was in a male surgical ward. I was alone with the patients as the other nurse had gone for her break. On this particular night, the hospital was short-staffed and there was not a relief person to help me out. This was quite often the situation. I had to deal with an emergency admission on my own, leaving the rest of the ward unattended. The admission was not the usual surgical patient, as beds were short across the rest of the hospital. We had a vacant bed that could be used as a temporary measure for the night.

The new admission was a man in his thirties. What I hadn't been told, because the duty doctor hadn't arrived with the notes, was that this patient had mental health issues. Minutes after the porters had delivered the patient and left the ward, the man pulled a sharp knife out of his trousers. It had a blade about six inches long. He had taken an instant dislike to the man in the next bed. Voices in his head were telling him to stab his neighbour.

The poor patient in the next bed was an elderly man with a broken femur. His leg was attached to a full ring Thomas splints with weights suspended off the end of the bed for traction. This was a mechanical device to stabilise the fracture. He was in the surgical ward as he also needed an abdominal operation. Helplessly tied to his bed with no means of escape, he became very frightened. I could not go for help just in case the new patient did stab him. I rationalised it was the elderly man he wanted to kill and not me, so I put myself between the two patients and held my ground, trying to calm the situation while the patient with mental health problems danced around brandishing his knife. I was not frightened as adrenaline had kicked into my system and I was desperate to protect the man tied to his bed with the splint on his leg. Other patients on the ward were now awake having heard the commotion. I asked one of them, who I knew to be ambulatory and sensible, to go for help. Much to my relief, after ten minutes, he came back with three porters who took care of the situation, and the offending patient was removed.

One nurse on another ward was not so lucky. It was the middle of the day, and as she was bending down to help a patient onto a bedpan, he grabbed her scissors out of her bodice pocket and stabbed her in the neck. The point of the scissors hit a major vessel, and she almost bled to death. She was rushed to the theatre for surgery. Eventually, she made a full recovery, although she was very traumatised. In another incident, I did end up being hit heavily in the jaw by a delirious patient who had recently had their leg amputated. The damage was bad bruising and dizziness but mostly hurt pride. I met with many other threatening and unpleasant sexual incidents during my nursing career.

On starting my nursing training, I was looking forward to living away from home and not being under the gaze of my parents. I had left behind the pointless rules and regulations of boarding school. I swapped all of that for a strict nursing training regime with fearsome nursing sisters, a formidable hospital Matron and consultant medical staff that could make you freeze with terror.

My training time at the RVI was a period in my life that I would describe as "burning the candle at both ends". As a student nurse, I worked and studied hard and was dedicated to the profession. Nonetheless, I was a teenager following an instinctive need to have fun and party. After all, it was the 1960s. Any thought of being adopted was overtaken by the desire to follow my career and meet boys.

During the first few weeks of my training, I made solid, lifelong friendships. Sixty years later, a group of about ten of us, meet every few months, and in an instant, we can revert to the fun of our student days. We readily exchange stories with lots of laughter and reminiscing. There are many hilarious incidents to recall, especially the parties.

Chapter 3

I t was at one of our many Saturday night student parties in Newcastle when I met my future husband, Peter. It was December 1964, and along with my flatmates, we were at a medics' party. The music was lively, the room was full of the sound of the early nineteen-sixties rock 'n roll. I was dancing with various people. Towards the end of the evening, I was with a wealthy medical student who had an MG Midget sportscar. He asked if he could give me a lift home. The horror of the lecture on how evil male medical students were, was impregnated in my mind, so I resisted even though it was a cold winter's night. Does the sanitary product representative realise she had such an effect on me that I would never date a doctor?

Little did I realise this was the best decision of my life, as waiting in the wings was Peter. He was watching and listening to my conversation with the medical student. He heard me say "no" to the offer of a lift home and then swooped in and asked me for the last dance. The song playing was "Save the Last Dance for Me" by the Drifters. It was that evening that I decided I wanted to see more of this tall, dark-haired, good-looking boy who escorted me on the twenty-minute walk back to my flat and never let go of my hand. Luckily, Peter did indeed ask me out on a date. We saw each other every other day for the next few weeks, which included Christmas and New Year. By New Year's Eve, I was smitten and in love with this six-foot-three rugby-playing student. Afterwards one of my friends said to me, "I hear you are going out with a boy who plays the guitar and rides a motorbike."

"No," I said, "he plays a banjo and has a scooter." Not so romantic, but who cares when you fall in love at the age of nineteen? Perhaps it took Peter a little longer for the deep love to develop.

After a year into our relationship, Peter's parents moved to Leeds from Newcastle, and he went with them. Peter came back to Newcastle most weekends to visit me and play rugby. We wrote copious letters to each other, which we still have, and they fill a small suitcase. However, the relationship was tested when Peter moved, yet again, to Birmingham and what he thought would be the "high life". Following two years of being together and diectly after one happy romantic weekend, a "dear John" letter came from Peter, ending our relationship. I was devastated and hadn't seen it coming. The bottom fell out of my world, I found the rejection so hard to take and I was miserable.

By now I had qualified as a State Registered Nurse and was working in anaesthetics. When Peter's letter came, I felt suicidal. I could not manage to work. We were allowed three days off work without a sick note. I took to my bed for those three days and cried and cried and cried. There had been earlier boyfriends where the relationships had finished, but somehow this one was a truly deep rejection. I found it hard to talk to anyone about it except my two closest girlfriends, Judith and Sheila, with whom I shared a flat. They got fed up with me moping around and I can't say that I blame them. I was miserable and boring. I was just going through the motions of surviving. Maybe there was something deep inside my make-up that brought back the feelings of rejection by my birth mother. I'm not sure, but the experience was certainly extremely emotionally painful. Perhaps it was just a normal reaction for anyone who was jilted. I knew Peter was still coming to Newcastle to play rugby, but he certainly was not coming anywhere near me or my friends.

After ten weeks of misery, I had a dream. It seemed different from my normal dreams and very vivid. I could not get this dream out of my head. As soon as I woke up, I excitedly told my flatmates about my dream.

It was a beautiful summer's day on a Friday morning when I described my dream to Judith and Sheila. By this time, I was working as a staff nurse in an operating theatre. I was on a late shift starting at one o'clock and finishing at nine in the evening. I explained to Judith and Sheila that in my dream I knew Peter was coming for the weekend to play rugby. He would be staying in the flat of his elder brother, who was a dental student and hadn't moved away from Newcastle to Leeds with his parents. The dream was detailed and very real. I dreamt that I went to Fenwick's, the department store in the centre of Newcastle. I bought a "washed denim look" pale pink cotton, slightly fitted, "A" line dress with a central zip three-quarters of the way down the front. It was sleeveless with two patch pockets in the skirt. I dreamt that after I had finished work, Peter met me at the hospital and said, "Shall we drive to Tynemouth and walk along the beach." My flatmates dismissed the dream as rubbish. Nevertheless, before I went to work, I did go to Fenwick's, and there was my pink dress on the end of a rail. It did not matter how much the dress cost, I did not even consider the price, especially when I tried it on, and it fitted perfectly. I was not entirely sure I believed in the premonition of my dream, but thought I deserved a treat anyway.

When I got to work, theatre was busy with the normal operating list. We were the "on-call" theatre for emergencies. Urgent cases were piling up to be done when the planned list had finished. I hardly had a break, let alone time to think about my dream. When I did get to take a short break at about seven o'clock in the evening, I realised I hadn't phoned my mother all week. I felt guilty so I dashed out to the public phone box on the hospital corridor and phoned home. I hadn't told my mother about my breakup with Peter as the whole episode was still too raw and I hadn't come to terms with the pain myself. I never shared anything too personal with my parents, but that was the norm in our household and that of a young girl.

The phone at home in Durham was in the hall, by a window that looked down the garden path. While I was chatting on the phone, my mother said that Peter was coming up the path to the front door and would I like to speak to him. At that time, Peter worked for Dunlop and several months before had promised to get my mother some latex pillows. My mother suffered from arthritis in her neck and shoulders with all her violin playing. She thought the new foam pillows would help and be more comfortable. Peter was delivering the pillows. As he entered the house, she handed the phone to him. He told me afterwards he was taken quite by surprise as he had no intention of contacting me. With my mother at his side listening to our conversation, he meekly asked what time I finished work. I told him and we arranged to meet just after nine o'clock at a side entrance to the hospital. Of course, I was dumbfounded and elated.

I rushed to find Judith and Sheila, who were also working late shifts, to let them know that Peter was meeting me after work. They did not believe me, and they took some persuading that my dream was coming true.

Peter did meet me from work; he was gracious enough not to stand me up. I was wearing my pink dress, which I knew suited me and I was confident that I looked good. Once in the car, he said, "Shall we drive to Tynemouth and walk along the beach?" I did not dare show how happy I was in case I frightened him off. We were both trying to play it cool. After that night, our relationship was back on track. The love and passion were even stronger than before. I never did tell my mother the story of how she was responsible for bringing us back together. Now I wish I had as she would have loved the scenario of my dream. She did have a belief in extrasensory perceptions and the untapped powers of the human mind.

Later that year, in 1967, I went to Leeds to study midwifery. Peter by then had moved to Sheffield, where, in time, I took up a post as a senior theatre sister. Between March and September of 1968, I had a six-month gap in my employment. I and two others decided to accept jobs as casualty nurses at a Butlins Holiday Camp in Pwllheli in North Wales for the summer season. The camp could accommodate 12,000 visitors with 1,500 staff. The three of us had just completed our midwifery course. A private company ran the holiday camp, so it was outside the National Health Service. In effect, I had entered the world of private medicine.

The medical centre where I would live was a separate single-storey building a little way from the rest of the chalet lines where the holidaymakers stayed. The building was basic, consisting of the main patient waiting area with a doctor's surgery and a clinical room accessed from the communal waiting room. Our workforce was six staff plus a retired visiting doctor from the local town. There were three of us from Leeds, a nurse from Mansfield and a cleaner, Vera, from London. We were supervised by a nursing sister, who had worked there every summer for years.

We manned the medical centre twenty-four hours a day. We staggered our meal breaks to ensure continuous cover for the surgery. One lunchtime I was left in the surgery with Vera, the cleaner, while everyone else went to the main camp dining room for their midday meal. It was the first week of the season, so the place was quiet. However, a man of about forty came in worried about his seventeen-year-old daughter. The daughter was in the next-door chalet to him, and they were on holiday together. He was a widower as his wife had died some years before. He was worried that his daughter hadn't left her chalet all morning and he could hear her being sick. She had locked herself in and would not open the door.

I promised the father that I would visit his daughter to see if I could help. I knocked on the daughter's chalet door. Initially, she would not let me in, but after a little persuasion, she unlocked the door and dived straight back into bed with the sheets pulled up to her chin. She was adamant that her father was not to be allowed into the room. She was a pretty girl with dark chin-length wavy hair. However, she looked pale and drawn. She was extremely rude, swearing at me and saying that she did not need a nurse and asked me to leave. She said that she had eaten fish and chips the night before which had made her sick. At Butlins, many of the holidaymakers were young and they drank in the "Blinking Owl" bar most evenings. The floor of this bar was usually swilling with beer and was somewhere I never wanted to frequent. I thought it was not the food that had made her sick but more likely the alcohol. After all, I had experienced the same in my student days in Newcastle.

I was happy to leave the chalet to let her deal with her hangover, thus avoiding more of the abuse that was coming my way. But how wrong could I have been? As I was leaving, I noticed a prescribed bottle of iron tablets on the chest of drawers. Now why, I thought, would a doctor prescribe iron tablets to a young girl? I sensed something was wrong. This girl was looking pale and huddled up in her bed with the blankets piled high. Not unusual as it was only March and still quite cold outside. I sat on the bed to try and have a chat with her, asking her, gently, broad questions about herself. She told me that every year she had been coming on vacation with her father to the same holiday camp ever since her mother had died. Her mother had died some six or so years previously. I decided to examine her abdomen as, at times, she seemed in pain and not at all comfortable. I managed to get her to release the bedclothes. I put my hand on a large extended uterus and then felt a contraction. This was not a hangover or food poisoning; this girl was about to have a baby. I could feel the baby's head well engaged and she was entering the delivery stage of labour. Did she know what was happening to her body? I asked her about her periods, which she had said were regular and the last one was about a week ago. It does happen, on rare occasions, that women can continue having periods throughout their pregnancy. Also, equally rare, young girls can be ignorant of their condition. There was not much time to waste and all I had in my pocket was a pen, paper and a thermometer, not a lot of use when delivering a baby. As gently as I could I told her she was about to have a baby.

At the next contraction, she admitted she knew what was happening but under no circumstances was I to tell her father. I did not have time to think about how that would play out and thought I would deal with that issue later. I wrote a note for Vera, who was back in the medical centre, asking her to bring the emergency bag. I instructed her to send, urgently, for the doctor to come straight to the chalet and to call an ambulance. Then she should find one of the other nurses to help me. I gave the note to the father and off he hurried. He had been waiting outside and was beside himself with anguish and was pleased to be given a task which would help his daughter. At that moment, the girl was my priority, so I decided to keep her secret as long as possible. I did not mention the baby in the note for fear the father would then find out what was happening.

In this situation, I thought the emergency bag might be of limited use. However, I did know that there would be an ampule of ergometrine, which would aid the contraction of the uterus after the baby was delivered. This would help the speedy passage of the placenta and reduce the risk of heavy bleeding as the afterbirth came away. Also, I would have the blood pressure machine and a stethoscope so that I could listen to the baby's heart rate and check the mother's blood pressure. The other nurses were still at lunch. Vera hadn't contacted them, thinking not a lot was happening and that it was something I could handle. The only help I had until the doctor arrived was Vera. Vera's role was a cleaner, she was squeamish and did not want to enter the chalet. So I gave her the task of keeping the father calm. She stayed outside chatting with him. He was still under the illusion that his daughter had food poisoning.

On examination, the baby in the womb was fine with a strong healthy heartbeat and showed no signs of stress. I estimated the delivery to be within the next fifteen minutes. However, the mother was a worry. Her blood pressure was sky-high, indicating pre-eclampsia. This is a dangerous condition for the mother as it can lead to organ failure and fits, and in turn, would put the baby at risk. It was important to get a healthy baby delivered as soon as possible. The doctor arrived just as the head was being delivered. He was also not well equipped for a delivery. Fortunately, I found the mother's nail scissors which, in anticipation, I had already scrubbed clean and boiled in the chalet kettle. Her hair ribbon was to hand. I used these to cut and tie the cord. We delivered a beautiful healthy baby girl. Sadly, the mother would not look at her baby. I wrapped the baby in a blanket and asked Vera to come into the chalet and hold this precious bundle.

Now it was time for me to explain to the girl's father what had happened. This was not an easy task as he had no inclination of his daughter's condition. She had hidden her pregnancy well under fashionable, large, oversized knitted jumpers. As the father digested the news, he was furious with me, making out that the whole pregnancy was my fault. When the ambulance arrived, I went with the mother and baby on the thirty-mile journey over bumpy roads to Bangor. My worry for the mother was acute, and I was relieved when we arrived at the hospital, and I could hand her over to the medical staff. She was immediately given medication and put into a darkened side ward on her own to rest. It was such a shame that after the delivery neither she nor her father would hold or even look at this perfect beautiful baby girl. The infant was put up for adoption. I felt so sad. Was this what it was like after my mother gave birth to me? Had she cared or was it just a case of getting the delivery over and done with so she could get back to her life without the burden of a baby?

It was not possible to talk to this young mother about her decision as she was too ill. Her father was in no mood to even contemplate a baby in the family. He was angry and confused and still giving me a load of grief. I did hear later that the girl made a good recovery physically. I suppose the only way she could cope emotionally was never to look at her baby so as not to form an attachment.

I rode back to Pwllheli with the girl's father, in the front of the ambulance. He verbally harassed me all the way. It was impossible to reason with him over the fact that he was now a grandfather. The poor ambulance driver drove in silence, fearing he would get the same abuse from the man if he joined in. I tried my best to get the father to be sympathetic towards his daughter's situation. As an adoptee, it hit home how I was once that innocent baby arriving in the world and then abandoned. Driving back in the ambulance, I had an enormous amount of empathy for this young mother and her baby. I was aware of an irresistible need growing inside me to work my way through the guilt and darkness of my own family's secrets to find my own identity.

Two years later, in 1970, my father married Peter and me in Durham Cathedral. My mother had worked hard to make the day perfect. It was a beautifully happy June day as we stood at the bottom of the chancel steps, looking up into the choir, while my father performed the ceremony. We were facing all our friends who were seated in the choir. The reception took place in Conrad Eden's house. He was the organist at the Cathedral. His house was in The College a few doors away from my home. After we were married, I had a new sense of belonging and I was desperate to have babies. This would mean that I would have a proper family tree and a new bloodline belonging to me and Peter.

In my life, my father only gave me three bits of advice. The first two areas of advice I found quite amusing. He told me never to pluck my eyebrows or to drink gin. What was it in his past that made him so knowledgeable about women's eyes or drinking gin? The final thing was more of a warning that came on my wedding day. He told me, "Don't think you can come back and ask me to marry you for a second time." Thankfully, I had no intention of breaking my vows to Peter. However, I did break my father's first two rules.

What I could not do, was talk to my parents about my adoption. Now I was a married woman. As an adult I sensed the time had passed as, sadly, I felt uncomfortable speaking to them about the circumstances of my birth. Tragically we never ask the most important questions of our parents.

Chapter 4

A year after we were married, Peter and I moved from Sheffield to York. York is where our three glorious children were born. I would have been devastated if I could not have had children. Where would that have left me floating in the world with no future and no past? Our first child, Stuart, was born in 1973 and in short succession, our other two children arrived. They were born at home, a girl Bridgette, and then another boy James. Having the family around me at home seemed to be the most natural way to give birth. It was also much more comfortable to have my own bathroom and to be able to eat whenever and whatever I felt like. Not having to make childcare arrangements was another reason for preferring a home birth.

When I gave birth to each of our three children, I tried to think what it would be like to give up my babies shortly after delivery. After the pain of labour and the sheer exhaustion of pushing a baby into the world, comes the love and ecstasy of cuddling the most precious tiny human being. It was unimaginable to think that my babies could have been taken from my arms for me to never see them again. I was deeply moved by the fact that these wonderful babies were biologically part of me. Stuart was the first person in the world that I met, who shared my genes. At this point,

I was able to appreciate the anguish of a mother having to give up a child. My birth mother must have been tormented when she handed me over for adoption. It's hard to imagine how she ever recovered from the intense emotional damage that she must have suffered. I could not dismiss the thought that she was more than likely affected by my birth for the rest of her life. The only way she could have coped would have been to condition her mind, early in her pregnancy, to the fact that the baby could never be hers. She must have been swayed by fear at the thought of the outrage from her parents. I'm so glad I never had to make that inconceivably distressing choice as to whether to keep my baby, give it away or terminate the pregnancy.

After we moved to York, I kept up my career as a theatre sister in the local hospital. I worked part-time during this period so that I could look after my family. When in York, Peter studied at Leeds University as a mature student. We were happy but broke. Most of our money went into paying the mortgage. This did not seem to worry us when we sold our two cars and ate carefully. We got by on my salary, child allowance and a mature student grant. We were lucky to have no university fees and the easy availability of well-paid summer work for Peter during the long holidays. Peter earned good money on each of the vacations, usually working on building sites in the summer and for a wine merchant over Christmas.

After completing a postgraduate year at York University, Peter secured a job as a trainee Prison Governor. Until the end of the first three-month module of his training, it was unknown where he would be posted. A house was to be provided with the job, so we decided to put our house in York on the market. It sold quickly and we invested our money into a canal narrow boat. The thinking behind this was that our family holidays would be sorted, and we could take the boat with us to Peter's various postings, given that the Prison Service often moved its managers.

The posting arrived in late 1976, but to our horror, it was the Isle of Wight where there were no canals within one hundred miles. However, undaunted, the boat came with us to Newport, the principal town on the island. Peter sailed the flat-bottomed eighteen-inch draught narrow boat across the Solent, into Cowes harbour and down the Medina River to Newport. We moored her up against the quayside, beside the old warehouses, in the centre of the town. We named her "Scumble". She became quite famous among the locals, as she was the only canal narrow boat the island had ever seen. At the time, a brewing company called Burt's had a business on the island. Peter painted the craft in the traditional narrow boat colours of red, yellow and green. A sign writer painted Burt's brewery logo on the side panels.

It was not until we were living on the Isle of Wight that I decided to actively research my adoption. Always nagging away in my mind was the mystery of my birth. The nudge to pursue my birth heritage was triggered by the fact that just before we left York in 1976, there was a change in the law. For the first time in England, Wales and Northern Ireland, adopted people, at the age of seventeen, were given the right to see their original birth certificate. In Scotland, this right had always been in place, and anyone over the age of sixteen had an automatic right to access their adoption papers. The adoption of children in England first became a legal process in 1926. Before this, formal adoption in England had remained a private matter, arranged mostly by volunteer charities. The Adoption of Children's Act of 1939 was not effectively enforced until after the Second World War. Independent adoption agencies were not brought under local authority control until 1949. The creation of the NHS in 1948 introduced methodical record-keeping. I was born in 1945.

Because of a strange sense of guilt, I found it hard to decide to send for my original birth certificate. I was delving into an area that was forbidden to me, because of hidden secrets. For a few years, I mulled the issue over and over in my mind. At the same time, I felt uncomfortable because of a sense of disloyalty to my parents in Durham. I had a belief that I was abusing the trust of the very people who had bought me up. However, I reasoned that I now lived a long way from Durham and there was no need to tell them what I was going to do.

In 1978, I wrote to the General Register office in Fareham, Hampshire, asking for a copy of my birth certificate. I always felt cheated, because all I had was an Adoption Certificate rather than what most people have, a Birth Certificate. For those adopted, the Adoption Certificate is the replacement for a birth certificate. It looks like a birth certificate, but across the top, mine had the words "Certified Copy of an Entry in the Adopted Children Register". Even if I obtained my original birth certificate, I could not use it as my official document to replace my adoption certificate. It's an awkward situation as my legal name is my adopted name.

To this day, the Adoption Certificate still must be used when starting a new job, getting married, applying for a passport and so on. I have a legitimate sense of disgruntlement in the fact that any clerk, in say a passport office, becomes privy to the fact that the person in front of them was adopted. I have a strong conviction that there must be a better way. It does not seem reasonable that adopted people can't use a birth certificate but are obliged to present an adoption certificate, although I do realise there has to be some reference to a change of name and parents.

The birth document should be designed so that various administrators are not privy to your birth circumstances. On my adoption certificate, the second column (the first being the entry number) shows the date when I was legally adopted, which in my case was a year after I was born. It does not show my place of birth but only the place where the Juvenile Court met and agreed that I was then lawfully adopted. It's not until the sixth column on the Adoption Certificate that my actual date of birth appears. When applying for a job once, I was asked by the confused office person checking my certificate, why I hadn't offered my birth certificate. I had to explain that my Adoption Certificate was the official substitute for my birth certificate, which I was legally obliged to submit.

Following my request to obtain my birth certificate, I was sent a letter from the Fareham office, in the county of Hampshire, asking me to complete an application form and pay the appropriate fee. After sending the form, I got a reply saying that I was to be allocated a counsellor. That seemed a bit insulting, given that I was thirty-three, yet needed to be counselled before obtaining my birth certificate. I went along with the bureaucracy as it was the only way I could get my hands on the certificate that I desperately wanted. I met the counsellor in a council office on the Isle of Wight, in a room that was only just big enough for a small table and two chairs. She was a pleasant woman, and she explained that she had to assess whether I understood the implications attached to securing my birth certificate. She also said that she needed to ensure that I was mentally stable to be able to receive the certificate.

The counsellor's conversation prompted the old feelings of guilt for even thinking of applying for my birth details in the first place. She said she would let me know her findings in due course, which felt like a further insult. My birthright lay in the hands of this woman. After several weeks, I heard from her telling me that she had my birth certificate. A meeting was arranged to hand over the long-awaited document. The counsellor was disappointed that I chose not to open the envelope, with the certificate in it, in front of her. I could not chance her seeing me becoming emotional, as she might snatch the document away, concluding that I was unsuitable and unbalanced. When I opened the document later, the condition of the certificate was insignificant and a bit disappointing. It was poorly printed on cheap, thin grey Xeroxed paper, it had a note tagged down the right side saying "adopted". There was no nice rolled-up scroll with a ribbon around it. My end-of-year school photo was better presented. This confirmed that the authorities were not paying any attention in recognising, that for me, it was a life-changing moment. I presumed they thought by sending a counsellor they had fulfilled their obligations.

The birth certificate confirmed my name as Donna Mary Hamilton. It showed who my birth mother was, and her home address of Edmonton, Alberta, Canada. Her occupation was a clerk in the Royal Canadian Air Force with a current address, at the time of registering my birth, of Alderbrook Park, Cranleigh, Surrey. There was no father's name. My adopted and lawful married name is Catherine Elizabeth Hamilton Atkinson, which is a strange coincidence because my birth mother's name was Elizabeth Hamilton. My adoptive mother always told me that she called me Elizabeth, after my godmother, and Hamilton was her family name. But perhaps, my birth name Hamilton influenced her decision when choosing which baby to adopt. It's now common for children to have some knowledge and mementoes of their pre-adoption heritage. It was quite the opposite when I was adopted in the 1940s. The common belief was it was best for all if the slate was wiped clean once the adoption had been agreed.

My place of birth was also a surprise. I was not born in Petersfield Hospital as my mother had always believed. I was born in a Canadian field hospital near Bramshott in Hampshire. Up until the point of receiving my birth certificate, I always used to say that I was born in Petersfield. Reading my certificate, I thought that an overseas wartime field hospital had a far more romantic ring to it. Even more exciting: I was born on Canadian soil.

After obtaining my birth certificate, I was able to apply, to the General Register Office for England, to request any information that the court records had on my adoption. When my Adoption Order arrived, it did not tell me anything new. It was one sheet of paper issued by the Juvenile Court of Bishop Auckland in County Durham. However, there was a mistake on the document that no one had noticed. Under the heading of the "date of the adoption order", it said 3 September 1945, which was eight days before I was born. I presume it should have said 3 September 1946. This was an error, but it illustrates the point that caution is sometimes needed when looking at historical legal documents.

When I was clearing out my mother's papers after she died in 1983, I came across an envelope. Written on the back of this empty reused envelope were the words: "Donna Mary Hamilton Sept. 11th. 1945, Elizabeth Jane Hamilton, Canadian Air Force.? (sic) Edmonton Alberta. Born at Petersfield Hospital. Father Canadian Air Force. National Children's Adoption Association". My mother had written that my father was in the Canadian Air Force. I still have the envelope. The only new piece of information was the first hint of who my father might have been.

After I received my birth certificate, further thoughts about my adoption took a back seat. I did not feel the need to discuss it with anyone other than Peter. Our lives were fulfilled and happy. Family, work and having a good social life took precedence. We were busy bringing up our children, I was working as a nurse in theatre, playing a lot of squash, attending night classes, and generally being involved with friends on the Isle of Wight.

Peter's next move, in 1980, took us to Stafford, which was perfect for our narrow boat as it was in the heart of the inland waterways system. I had reluctantly given up the nursing career which I had loved. The NHS much preferred nurses who worked full-time, and with a young family, this was difficult. Often, part-time highly qualified nurses were made to feel like recruits and given posts far below their experience and qualifications. NHS employers were slow to recognise the value of married women wanting to continue their careers by working part-time. Consequently, over many decades, nurses dropped out of the profession, including me. It was a hard decision to make but was born out of necessity. It was impossible to balance family life and three children and work full time as an "on-call" theatre sister. Rather than feeling unfulfilled in my nursing profession, I decided to change careers.

Our move from Stafford in 1982 took us to Wakefield, where we sold the boat and bought a house. The Prison Service wanted to reduce its housing stock and was keen that employees buy their own properties. The boat had served its purpose, providing us with lots of family holidays and weekends away. It was now time to cash in the asset and put the money into a house of our own. We bought a four-bedroom end terrace in the village of Walton on the outskirts of Wakefield. We were happy, healthy and contented. The children went to the village school. We built up a good social life and again took up squash, and swam at Walton Hall Spa hotel, ten minutes' walk from the house.

I began an academic course in textile design and technology. I studied at Bradford College, Harrogate College of Art and finally at Leeds University. I worked late into the night after the children were in bed, learning all about hydrogen bonds and other such chemical reactions related to the performance of fibres, dyes and fabrics. I also enjoyed a module on computer programming which was necessary to keep pace with the evolving design technology. I became a successful freelance textile designer, which meant that I could work from home with the odd week away in London, Europe and New York to sell my work. But our organised comfortable family life was about to change.

Part 2:

—

Sadness and Heartbreak

Chapter 5

S uddenly, our lives took a terrible turn, and even after almost forty years, I find it far from easy to write these words. It was Easter weekend 1985, when I had a second vivid dream, this time about our 12-year-old son Stuart. I don't know how somebody can recall something in a dream that has yet to happen, and it then unfolds in precise reality. The subject of this dream could not have been more different from my earlier dream about Peter. This dream was stark, frightening, and profoundly disturbing.

I dreamt in clear detail that Stuart had to have his leg amputated. It was no dream conjured up with the benefit of hindsight, or something that I imagined after the event. It was explicit and truly horrible and was stuck in my head when I woke.

In my dream, I can distinctly recall scrutinising a consent form, which said the operation was for a leg amputation. I queried the reason behind this drastic action but was compelled by both the insistence of the nurse and the urgency of the situation that an operation to remove his leg was necessary. Whilst examining this form, I woke suddenly and tried to persuade myself it was only a dream. I tried to get it out of my mind. But every time I slid back to sleep, the same dream recurred and acted out as before. When I went to sleep, over the next couple of weeks, the dream repeated itself like some kind of haunting. I recounted the dream to Peter and his brother, to try to exorcise it from my thoughts, and if their memory is good enough, they will remember me telling them. Eventually, after about a fortnight, I did manage to persuade myself it was silly to keep dwelling on what was simply a dream.

However, some months after my dream, Stuart fell off his skateboard and bumped his right knee. It was painful and swollen. I took him to see our local doctor who prescribed anti-inflammatory drugs and rest. After a week of no improvement, an X-ray was organised at Pinderfields Hospital in Wakefield. The appointment was on a Monday afternoon. We went into the X-ray room and nine sets of pictures were taken, after which we were told to sit in the waiting area. We waited and waited whilst all the other patients left, having been told to see their GP. We were the last ones remaining in the waiting area, and I asked if we could go. The answer was, "Please hang on a bit longer." Then I overheard the radiographer talking on the phone to whom I presumed was the radiologist, who was the qualified person to examine and report on the X-rays. The radiographer came out and said that we must see our GP as soon as possible. More than a degree of worry had built up that something was wrong, as this was not the normal procedure. The radiographer would not pass on any further information.

Two days later, on the Wednesday, I had an appointment to see our GP. He was non-committal. He told me that he had made an appointment for Stuart to see an orthopaedic consultant on the Friday. He did tell me that the X-ray had shown that the problem was not to do with an injury but that there were "bone changes". Over the next twenty-four hours or so, I convinced myself that adolescent boys of Stuart's age often do have problems with knees and bone growth. I rationalised it could be a cartilage problem or something to do with his ligaments, patellar or tendons, or an infection, or even to do with the growth plates at the end of his femur. Physically active boys between the ages of ten and fifteen can develop Osgood-Schlatter disease, especially after a spurt of growth. Stuart was tall for his age. This would heal in time with a good outcome. It all fitted Stuart's profile. I was not prepared for what came next.

I took Stuart to see Mr Robson, the orthopaedic consultant at Pinderfields Hospital in Wakefield on the Friday. He casually chatted with Stuart and was charming. He then asked Stuart to wait outside while he talked to me. I was sitting on a chair next to his desk when Mr Robson got down on both knees in front of me. He said he was sorry to have to tell me that Stuart had cancer. He was a big man, like a front-row forward rugby player. His gesture of talking to me on his knees conveyed a huge amount of empathy, as though he was trying to minimise his size and his medical authority and connect with me as a normal person. He showed me the X-ray. Sure enough, there was a shadow showing a sarcoma. I was in shock, wanting to cry and scream out, "No, no, no, there must be some mistake." I did say something like, "Are you sure this is Stuart's X-ray?" Of course, it was Stuart's. Mr Robson was honest and definite about how poor the prognosis was.

In my heart, and with my nursing experience, I knew it was bad. Stuart was in the waiting room, and I had to go out and put a smile on my face as if nothing was wrong. The tension inside me was wanting to burst out. I just wanted to cuddle him and explain what was going to happen to his short life. This was the boy who first made us parents and was part of my genetic makeup. This was the boy who we sat in a baby chair on the table while we ate our meals and just stared and giggled at him. This was the boy about whom we felt such pride. This was the boy who was doing so well at school and had such imagination and flair. Horrible things could not happen to this beautiful child. That day at the hospital I could not break down in front of him, but I could not trust myself to control my emotions. We were going to set off on a regime of treatment and I had to be positive and give Stuart and the rest of the family hope that we would get through this. At that point, I felt I had become two people, I was divided in half. One half was a mother dreading what was happening to Stuart, and the other was the nurse telling herself to be strong and guide both Stuart and the family through what was to come.

By the time we left the hospital, it was late morning, and Peter was working at the Prison Service College in Wakefield as a management tutor. I knew he would shortly be on his lunch break, so I decided to take Stuart to see him. A secretary entertained Stuart in another room while I told Peter what had happened. Peter is the eternal optimist and did not take in the gravity of what I was telling him. He thought that the treatment would be difficult, but it would be all right eventually. But I knew from the start that no amount of treatment would make this dreadful disease go away.

I went back home with Stuart to find that a neighbour had left, on the doorstep, some strawberries which we both loved. That ended up being our lunch, after which Stuart wanted to go back to school for the afternoon. Although I did not want to let him out of my sight, I was happy for him to return to school. I needed time to weep such agonising tears and to think about how I was going to cope with what the consultant had told me. I wanted to protect Stuart and help him get through what lay ahead. Up to that point, it was the worst day of my life, and I knew there would be many more horrific, worse days to come. Shortly, the three children would be home from school and Peter back from work for the weekend, and then on the Monday, Stuart would be admitted to the hospital to have a confirmatory biopsy of his right femur. I was trying not to be pessimistic, but I knew how deadly this cancer was. No matter how I approached it, I could not see a way that our son could come out the other side of this. Peter could not take in the enormity of what he was facing. Then why should he, with no medical background?

Stuart went to theatre just before lunchtime for the biopsy to be performed. After the operation was over, Mr Robson came onto the ward to say that it did not look good and there was no reason to change his opinion on the initial diagnosis. Stuart's leg was painful, and the pain-killing drugs made him sick. His leg was splinted, and it was to stay like that until major surgery could be performed. There was the fear of a pathological fracture. It was hard to see Stuart suffering so much. We had explained to Stuart what was happening and that he had a tumour in the lower end of his femur. He was a bright boy and understood what we were saying. He accepted it was going to be a difficult road ahead. The pragmatism and optimism of youth is amazing, and he gave me the strength to cope with my distress.

Mr Robson offered a certain amount of hope, but his knowledge of this kind of cancer must have made him have serious doubts. He had arranged for us to see the oncology specialist at Cookeridge Hospital in Leeds to start chemotherapy. Dr Dave Boyd was to be our paediatric oncology consultant.

On Thursday 1 August 1985, we should have been going on a family holiday to a villa in Salema on the Portuguese Algarve. Instead, we were in an ambulance on our way to see Dave Boyd and the oncology team at Leeds. Stuart came to trust him, and they built up a good relationship. It was suggested to us that, after chemotherapy, a surgeon called Mr Mead in Birmingham, might be able to replace part of Stuart's femur and knee with a prosthesis.

A week later, Stuart was admitted to Ward 15 at St James's Hospital Leeds, for his first lot of chemotherapy drugs. The drugs were highly toxic, but they offered a small chance of disrupting the progress of his cancer. It was horrible for Stuart as he was so ill, he had such a bad reaction to severe sickness. I remember him asking me not to bring a drink of coffee near his bed because his sensitivity to smells made him want to retch. This regime of drugs was administered every third week via an intravenous drip in the hospital.

When I took Stuart back to St James's Hospital for his second round of drugs, he was extremely agitated. He now knew, as soon as the drip went up, how ill he was going to feel. The dread of being nauseous and befuddled while vomiting and being incontinent, made him scared and panicky. The sedative that he had been given on the first round had made the sickness almost unbearable. A houseman, called Tom, was particularly patient with Stuart and they liked each other. Tom was able to draw out from Stuart exactly how he was feeling. They agreed that, on this occasion, the sedative that caused so much sickness would be dropped, just sticking with the anti-sickness medication. This would hopefully help settle Stuart. He responded quite well and had a reasonable night's sleep but unfortunately, by the next day, which was my fortieth birthday, he reacted to the anti-sickness drug. From then on, he preferred to have the chemotherapy without the sedative and anti-sickness drugs. Although Stuart was feeling so ill, he managed a smile and wished me happy birthday. There was even a card on the locker that he had organised beforehand. How many more bad days could Stuart have? But inevitably there would be more.

We organised many fun moments and as a family, we tried to keep an optimistic, playful mood. Peter came into his own here, as that kind of approach was one of his strengths. As

August moved into September, Stuart, as expected, started to lose his hair. Nowadays, a young boy would just shave his head, and no one would think anything of it, but in 1985 that was far from the fashion. Young pop singers had long flowing hair and baldness was not necessarily a good look. There was an exception – Errol Brown, the lead singer and songwriter for the band "Hot Chocolate", was bald.

A few weeks after his hair had gone, we picked up a specially made wig from Leeds. Stuart was polite and said nothing to the wig lady who was proud of her handiwork. But as we were driving out of Leeds, past the Tetley Brewery, the passenger window opened and out flew the wig. Stuart wanted to have nothing to do with this hairy rat that had been carefully designed for his head. I stopped the car and retrieved it, but from then on, it went into the dressing-up box. Stuart thought that a baseball cap was a better look.

We were being carried along on a wave of hospital visits and treatments. Everyone was kind and positive and I almost believed the drugs would work. The never-ending regime of drugs and blood tests was so cruel and pushed us all to a point that we found exhausting. Stuart's sickness was unrelenting, and he had a bad reaction to every drug that was given to him. The days rolled into one of endless worry. During all this time, his knee remained splinted, swollen and immensely painful. Our two other young children, Bridgette and James, were brilliant and so patient, wanting to help in whatever way they could. On the few days when Stuart was feeling better, we tried to do lots of enjoyable things and have days away. We all deserved a break from the endless talk of hospitals and drugs.

Chapter 6

In early September 1985, just two months after Stuart's diagnosis, we went to Birmingham to meet Mr Mead, the orthopaedic consultant. Another biopsy was arranged for the hospital to size up for a possible replacement knee. Once back from Birmingham, it looked to me that Stuart's leg was getting worse and there seemed to be little sign of the tumour reducing after the first two sessions of chemotherapy. I could tell that the oncology doctor at Leeds was equally worried. It was decided to get Stuart back to Birmingham as soon as possible.

Stuart and I set off to drive to Birmingham from Wakefield, early on the morning of Monday 30 September. It was misty and we got stuck in four separate traffic jams. I was offered a small room in the Elizabeth Cadbury House, in the grounds of the Birmingham Royal Orthopaedic Hospital, whilst Stuart was in the children's ward. He was impressed that Ian Botham, the England cricketer, had also had a knee operation in the same hospital. This helped him settle and put his trust in the doctors.

The next morning, Mr Mead did his ward round and examined Stuart, followed by a private chat with me. Just as I suspected, Mr Mead thought the tumour had gone rampant and that the only way forward was an amputation as soon as possible. However, he thought there was a slight chance that the swelling showing on the

X-ray might be necrosis of the tissues surrounding the tumour. The drugs may have been doing their job after all. In those days, MRI scans were not routinely available. I worried and questioned that if the drugs had been ineffective, where would we go from here? Mr Mead said that if the tumour is large, then any more drugs will not touch it, but at least they might prevent any metastasis from developing. The operation was booked for the morning of the following Thursday.

Stuart was aware that he would have a blood transfusion during the surgery. He had picked up from the press about a blood scandal involving hepatitis C. This arose from infected donors giving their blood which could then pass the disease to patients. This was a worry for Stuart, even though the hospital tried to allay his fears. He wanted me to donate my blood but sadly we were different blood groups, making this not possible. I would have donated my whole body to Stuart, in a trice, if it could rid him of this cancer.

There was an older boy, aged fifteen, called Howard, who was in the bed opposite Stuart. They got on well. Howard's leg had been amputated from mid-thigh. He was like a role model to Stuart. However, Howard was discharged from the hospital the day before Stuart's operation was due to take place. The evening before Stuart was having his operation, he asked me what it would be like to have a leg amputated. I took this opportunity to explain to Stuart that he might well lose his leg. I had to tell him, the stark reality of what might happen. It was an awful shock to him, and we both cried, hugging, for a long time. He tried to reject what I was saying, suggesting that I was being horrible to him, he could not take in such an awful event happening. We talked and talked, and he calmed down enough to resign himself to the likelihood of an amputation. The ward sister was good, and together we went through all the positive ways of coping with a false leg. Earlier that evening Mr Mead had visited Stuart to tell him about his operation, but he never mentioned a possible amputation. All he talked about was that his knee prosthesis had been specially made for him by Stanmore Implants in Middlesex. I could not blame Mr Mead for ducking the most extreme outcome of the impending operation, but I thought Stuart needed to be aware of the prospect of an amputation. What if this optimistic boy woke from his operation and found he had no leg, then how bad would that be? And how would he trust any of us again?

That same evening, Peter was coming down by train to be with us for the operation. A friend took him to Wakefield station, and before the train left, she gave him a heartfelt hug – she knew he would need every bit of loving support he could get. He was going to stay, with me, in the hospital accommodation, then to be with Stuart for a few days. The plan was that I would go back home, after Stuart had recovered from the surgery, to spend a few days with Bridgette and James.

I wanted Peter to arrive in time to sign the anaesthetic consent form for Stuart's operation, but his cross-country train was delayed. The ward sister kept coming to me to get the form signed and I kept making excuses, thinking Peter would arrive any minute. Eventually, the sister said to me that she could not put off the signing any longer, as it was late, and she was going off duty. This then forced me into having to put my signature on the piece of paper, confirming an operation for either a knee replacement or an amputation. There was my dream staring me in the face. I desperately tried to avoid following the course of my dream that I had had six months before, but I could not. It was in my mind that if I did not sign this piece of paper, then Stuart would get a new knee and avoid an amputation. But it felt destined that the amputation would happen. I was left with no choice but to go along with my dream from the previous Easter. Re-enacting what had so disturbed me all those months ago was a crippling pain that left me drained of emotional energy. I could not believe this was happening. I'm not superstitious, and I don't believe in psychic powers or the supernatural, so I'm at a complete loss to understand how two dreams became reality in such detail.

Peter arrived late, but just in time to say goodnight to Stuart. By this stage, Stuart had settled and was no longer exercised by the prospect of what might happen the next day. We sat with him until he fell asleep. In the morning, Stuart was marvellous and was positive about his operation. Overnight he had accepted he was going to have a false leg. He was so brave and cheerful before he was taken into theatre. Peter and I went as far as the theatre doors to be with him for as long as we could.

Once the operation began, we went back to the Elizabeth Cadbury House to await the outcome. After a while, the ward sister phoned to tell us they could not replace the knee, and Mr Mead was amputating Stuart's leg. I just wanted to scream the place down, it was so awful. I could quite easily have let myself collapse into a heap of despair, but of course, this would not help anyone, let alone our son. Peter and I held each other tight and what little strength there was in each of us might combine enough to get us through. It was a horrible thought that part of our beautiful, perfect firstborn child was going to end up in a hospital incinerator.

We went to see Stuart in the recovery ward. He was an incredible patient. He made such a good instant recovery, thanks to an excellent anaesthetist, Dr Hall Davies, who happened also to be the Queen's anaesthetist. As soon as Stuart was conscious, I told him that his leg had gone. He answered in a matter-of-fact tone and said, "Yes, Mum, I know. It's OK." After a few minutes, the recovery ward sister came over and said that she needed to tell Stuart about the amputation. I replied that I had discussed it with him the night before and that he already knew. She was a bit annoyed with me and said it was her job to tell the patients and that I could not have told him as he would be in a "meltdown" with the news. She told me this is what normally happened in the recovery ward. It was their policy not to come clean with the children before the operation. That might be all right for other children, but it was not the way for our son.

I went back home to Wakefield to be with Bridgette and James while Peter stayed, for the weekend, in Birmingham. I was so pleased to see our other two children, who were eleven and nine, and to give them lots of hugs and reassurance. Our neighbours, friends, Stuart's Godmother Auntie Rena and Peter's parents were all a great support. My parents had died two years earlier. On Monday morning, I drove back to Birmingham in time for Peter to get the train home to be there for Bridgette and James coming out of school.

Stuart's progress was rapid. I was so proud of his bravery in getting on with his exercises in his nonchalant and easygoing manner. The only problem was I struggled to get him to eat proper meals. He had a thing about hospital food which started when he was undergoing his chemotherapy, triggered by his heightened sense of smell. Five days after Stuart's operation, an old flatmate and bridesmaid of mine, Judith, came to stay at the hospital. This was a great distraction for both Stuart and me. With Stuart in a wheelchair, the three of us 'escaped' and went to McDonald's in Northfield, near to the hospital. I'm not a particular fan of fast-food beef burgers, but I had to accept that this one tasted so good. Such a small thing gave Stuart immense pleasure, and it was lovely to see him relaxed and happy. We did not dare tell the ward where we had been as they would have worried about infection.

After the operation, Stuart remained in Birmingham for a week or so. Just before we were due to go home, I came onto the ward one morning from my little room at the Elizabeth Cadbury House, to find Stuart missing from his bed. I found him in the adjoining partitioned-off part of the ward, talking to some of the girls who had undergone operations themselves. The boys and girls were separated by a seven-foot divider sectioning off the two areas. All the boy patients had been discharged and Stuart felt lonely. He climbed the partition with his one leg and was sitting on one of the girl's beds, chatting to them without a care. He was gregarious, and being on his own when he could hear chatter close by, made him want to join in.

By the time we left the hospital in Birmingham, Stuart was coping well. When we arrived home, it was comforting and reassuring to have all the family back under one roof. Even today I still have that feeling of contentment when my children and grandchildren are all sleeping safely together in our house.

Stuart had a new lease of life and was animated as he could now move around pain-free. The leg which had given him so much agony was gone, and any post-operative discomfort was easy to cope with compared to the tumour pain. One of the first things he did was to try to ride his sister's bike. He longed for that feeling of movement and speed after being immobile for several months. This freedom and feeling of well-being was not to last though, because he had to return to the hospital in Leeds for six more rounds of chemotherapy.

The histology report on the leg identified the exact type of tumour, which was different from what had originally been thought. It was a Myxoid Malignant Fibrous Histiocytoma, a soft tissue sarcoma, which is a rare tumour in adolescents. It affected the connective tissue at the lower end of Stuart's right femur. Peter hated the fact that the tumour had a name, preferring to think of it as a horrible alien intrusion that did not deserve the dignity of a title. The conclusion was that the earlier chemotherapy drugs would have had no effect on the tumour. It was quite depressing to think that the drugs that had made Stuart so ill had been completely ineffectual. Stuart was now starting from scratch on a new set of drugs. This round of treatment would be completed, hopefully by the following May of 1986.

For the rest of the autumn term, a home tutor was organised for Stuart, which proved to be unsatisfactory. It turned out that Stuart's level of maths was more advanced than the tutor's. When I went into the room to listen to his tutorial sessions, Stuart was teaching the tutor rather than the other way around. She invariably arrived late and looked for any excuse just to have a chat over a cup of coffee. There was a feeling that she had written Stuart off as being a cause that was not worth the bother. Stuart was a bright child, with a love of learning and a thirst for knowledge. I spoke to his school, Crofton High School, and they agreed to set work for him and let him attend classes whenever he could manage. His class teachers were brilliant and bent over backwards to help wherever they could. He was happier among his friends and peer group. Often, he would spend his time in the school library and his various subject teachers would come and plan work for him. Stuart flourished academically and soon was ahead of his year group, especially in maths. He was a sociable child, and it was important for him to feel part of the school environment and to be in touch with his classmates.

We were sent to Chapel Allerton Hospital in Leeds for limb fitting. In 1985 the limbs were designed around elderly immobile patients and held in place with heavy belts and straps. This was no good for an active, twelve-year-old boy. However, the head of prosthetics, Mr Parker, did arrange for Stuart to have a lightweight limb weighing just two kilograms. When Stuart's mid-thigh stump was properly healed, there was the promise of a newly designed suction socket leg, which did away with the need for belts and straps. With no fuss, Stuart soon got used to walking on his artificial leg and he tried to play football with his cousins. It was admirable the way he coped with his phantom pains and the electric shocks that were an inevitable side effect of having a missing leg. Many people who did not know Stuart well had no idea that he had an artificial leg.

The subsequent rounds of chemotherapy were horrible for Stuart, as again he was sick, and his appetite was worryingly poor. I was anxious about his diet, as once again, his heightened sense of smell made him nauseous when food appeared. I tried many high-protein diets to build up his strength. During the weeks he was in hospital, having his intense sessions of chemotherapy, it made me deeply sad that I could not protect him or minimise his pain and anxiety. As both a nurse and a mother it was hard to sleep at night as I felt inadequate and helpless.

Sometimes Stuart became so fed up with what was happening to him that it was difficult to keep him motivated to continue with the gruelling treatment regime. During Stuart's better weeks between chemotherapy, we went swimming. He was a good club swimmer before the cancer, having competed for Wakefield Swimming Club. Even with only one leg to propel himself along, he could beat me with ease.

I devised a scheme to count off each hospital visit by putting a row of secret, wrapped presents on a shelf in his bedroom, like opening a Christmas Calendar. Every time he came home from his chemotherapy, he was excited to open his small present. Also, he was keen to try his hand at simple computer programming. We had an Acorn BBC Microcomputer that used BASIC as its language. There were games that he played on this early computer. The ones I remember were Planetoid and Space Invaders.

Chapter 7

S tuart's chemotherapy marched on, and we were now into the New Year of 1986, a year we thought might bring hope and optimism with a change for the better. Peter and I used to take it in turns to travel from our home in Wakefield to St James's Hospital in Leeds to sit with Stuart late into the evening. I did the daytime session and Peter did the evenings. One night, in early January, Peter came out of the hospital at just after ten at night to find our car had been stolen. Stuart's godmother, Auntie Rena, lived in Leeds, and she ran Peter home after the police were informed. The car was found the next morning, beside a high-rise block of flats with the battery removed. There was no other serious damage, but our camera had been stolen holding all our family Christmas and New Year undeveloped photographs. Also, a pair of new trainers, which were still in their box, were taken. They were a present for Stuart. We wondered what type of person wanted to steal cars from a hospital car park.

We had a super, relaxed, and happy Christmas holiday. Peter took time off work and Stuart was feeling good between his chemotherapy treatments. His hair was beginning to grow, and he was putting on weight. We went to stay with friends in Sheffield and because of plenty of snow we went sledging, but the photographs from this period were now all lost. This was thanks to the person who broke into our car. Our family Christmas photographs could not be replaced. Why did the person not take the car and leave the photos?

Over the next months, the chemotherapy treatment was on its three-week schedule, a remorseless round of sickness and discomfort. The regime involved about five days in hospital, followed by a two-week gap. Two weeks was just enough time for Stuart to start feeling normal and get his appetite back. Then the unremitting painful schedule would start all over again with the poisonous cocktail being pumped into his veins.

Stuart turned thirteen in January 1986 and for some time Peter hadn't been well. He was being treated at Pinderfields Hospital, Wakefield, for a urinary infection. All along I was not convinced that this was the correct diagnosis, and suddenly his illness came to a head a few weeks before Easter. On his visit to the doctor, I told him to tell his GP that it was not a urinary infection but appendicitis. Sure enough, he ended up as an emergency admission with a burst appendix and an abdominal abscess. It was too dangerous to operate, so he stayed in the hospital for a week on an antibiotic drip. His appendix was to be removed at a later date. Our plans for a nice Easter holiday went out of the window. Peter came out of the hospital just in time for me to take Stuart back to Leeds for his fifth and penultimate set of chemotherapy drugs.

Stuart wore his "new leg" most days, it now had a suction socket mechanism, and he quickly mastered the walking technique. It was the latest model and designed to mimic a real leg. It was padded and shapely and covered in a flesh-coloured "wipe clean" material. The design was more like an adult female leg than that of a teenage boy. Today's "bionic" legs would have been more suitable for Stuart, but we had the best available in the 1980s. One day in the late afternoon, we went to a friend's house for a family party. Many of our friends were there as well as some people we did not know. After a while, Stuart's artificial leg was becoming uncomfortable, and the suction socket mechanism had come loose. I sat Stuart down and without really thinking about those around us, I got hold of his mechanical ankle and pulled. The leg easily slipped out from under his jeans. The gasps of horror from those close by were audible. For a split second, they thought I had torn off my son's leg from his body. I sat down next to Stuart with the leg on my knee and we had a good giggle.

Stuart was desperate to ride his bike, but with his artificial leg being on the right, this meant he could not use the right pedal. The fixed ankle was the problem, as was the restricted articulation of the artificial knee joint when it came to turning the pedal. For him to be able to ride a normal bike, several technical adjustments would be necessary. We found a cycle shop in Harehills in Leeds, that supplied machines to top national riders, one of whom was Beryl Burton. She was from Leeds and was a road and track champion cyclist having won seven world titles.

A special bike was built for Stuart with a crank for the gears on the left side that could be powered by his left foot. Initially, they said that there was a six-month waiting period, but when I explained the situation, they sorted the bike within a week. They built it with a Dawes frame, and it had a fixed right pedal to accommodate Stuart's artificial leg. This meant that he would always have to remember that when he stopped, he would need to put his left foot to the ground. The issue was that his right false foot was strapped tightly onto the pedal and could not easily be released.

Stuart managed his bike surprisingly well and quickly got used to riding at speed. I worried that if he fell to the right into the traffic, he would not be able to save himself by putting his foot on the ground. One day along with Peter, Bridgette and James, he rode from Wakefield and back, to visit his grannie, Peter's mother, in Leeds. That was a round trip of about thirty miles. Not bad for a thirteen-year-old boy with only one leg after having undergone extensive chemotherapy.

Chapter 8

T he elation of the new bike and the celebration of the end of the chemotherapy ended abruptly. In May 1986, Peter, Stuart and I went to Seacroft Hospital in Leeds for a routine blood test and a chest X-ray. To everyone's sorrow and our complete horror, two tumours were found, one in each lung. Before his leg was amputated, the tumour had thrown off some seeds which had circulated and come to rest in his lungs.

There was still a glimmer of hope. Dr Boyd arranged for Stuart to be admitted the next day to the hospital. By Thursday, he was in theatre having major chest surgery to remove the tumours, by means of a sternotomy. A long incision was evident down the centre of his chest. He recovered well and was home and in good spirits within days. I was in a state of shock as I knew the cancer had thrown off metastasis. That was not supposed to have happened. The chemotherapy and the leg amputation were meant to have prevented the metastasis.

We had booked to go to London for three nights to celebrate the end of the chemotherapy treatment, but we had to cancel. In the meantime, Peter was back in the hospital to have his appendix removed; he did well and was quickly home. We rearranged the trip to London, including a theatre performance, for July.

The cruellest thing for Stuart was that we had to keep him away from his bike until his chest had healed. The very thing that gave him so much pleasure and the joy of experiencing speed, had to be withheld.

The rearranged weekend in London was a wonderful, well-deserved break for us all. The children loved Trafalgar Square. We have memorable photographs of them sitting together on the lions around Nelson's column. As soon as he could, after his chest surgery, Stuart went back to school for the rest of the summer term. He got a glowing end-of-year report and was top of his year.

Over the summer and into the autumn, we took every opportunity to enjoy ourselves and give the children as many happy memorable times as we could. We had days out, and we went camping at Alton Towers theme park. We also had a short break at the mock Italian village of Port Merrion in North Wales. We stayed in the Lakes at our favourite cottage near Loweswater. Stuart insisted that he could climb mountains, so we all went up Mellbreak, a small mountain near the cottage. He managed well with his artificial leg and limited lung capacity. On the way down, Peter got him to sit on a large piece of slate and slid him down a scree for part of the descent. We walked up through Mosedale Valley at the west side of Mellbreak over to Ennerdale. Stuart was exhausted but exhilarated by his achievement. We took our bikes to the Lakes, which gave Stuart a lot of pleasure. It was a joy to see that Bridgette and James continued to be so patient and supportive of their brother. They were amazing children throughout the whole of Stuart's illness, and we were so proud of them, especially being only eleven and ten at the time. But of course, they did not fully appreciate the extreme gravity of Stuart's illness.

Just when we thought things could get no worse, an X-ray in early August showed five more new lung tumours. The chemotherapy had failed and there was no point in any further operations. The results were devastating, and the doctors could not help Stuart anymore. He had only a few more months to live. Although I was expecting this outcome, I still could not believe what was happening. Dying only happened to patients I nursed, not to my firstborn child. The gravity of the situation made Peter and me sit in numbed silence. We did not want to speak. We felt no need to ask questions because we knew only too well that nothing could save Stuart now.

The doctors and the nursing staff at Leeds remained hugely supportive and they were not going to abandon Stuart. They were able and willing to go on helping us as a family through the final months of Stuart's life. He was upbeat and happy by nature, and it was obvious that he wanted to enjoy his life despite what he was going through. He knew he had cancer, and he knew people died of cancer, but he never actually vocalised that it may be him who would not make it. I had this conversation with him on several occasions, usually sitting on the stairs at home. I always found that sitting on the stairs was a good place to resolve issues.

The medical team at Leeds wanted me to explain to Stuart, in stark terms, that he would shortly die. They said that if I did not tell him they would. By this time there was another consultant on the team, Alistair Long, whom we all liked, and Stuart felt comfortable and relaxed in this company. He was a kind, gentle person who looked like a giant teddy bear. However, I had one terrible meeting with the staff who I had trusted throughout Stuart's treatment. They stressed that their policy was to be brutally honest with Stuart about his prognosis. As his parent, I responded that I did not share their strategy, and I had no intention of spelling out such disaster to our optimistic and feisty boy. Peter and I were totally at one with this. I told them, we would, as a family, deal with the issue in a way we believed to be in the best interests of our child. Peter and I were his parents, we knew our child and neither of us was in denial as to what was about to happen. If we, as parents, could carry the burden of his pending death, it was the least we could do.

It was strange as on the one hand the hospital in Birmingham would not approach Stuart to tell him he might have to have his leg amputated, but in Leeds, they wanted to spell out to him that he was about to die.

I approached the subject of dying with Stuart, and he said he understood but did not want to talk about it further. The door was always kept ajar for him to ask questions, but it was obvious he wanted to handle his illness on his terms. It was hard to accept that the team of caring professionals took a united stand in forcefully pressurising me into doing something that we so adamantly thought was wrong for our family. They had me in tears at one meeting as they kept pressing the point. The team was made up of doctors, nurses, a counsellor and a social worker. Peter and I had no intention of destroying Stuart's remaining few months by telling him that he would not be with us on Christmas Day to open his presents.

For the first half of the autumn term in 1986, Stuart remained well, but of course, the tumours were still growing in his chest. We still had pressure from the Leeds medical team to tell Stuart that he was dying, but he seemed so happy and positive and enjoying life. We felt that no good would come from having to spell it out to him. He was thirteen, he had no will to write, and he was surrounded by a loving family and supportive peer group friends. How could we let Stuart go to sleep each night worrying that he may not wake up in the morning? There was a local Macmillan nurse who was fantastic.

She helped Stuart, as well as Peter and me, by encouraging us to go with our instincts and do what we felt was right for our son. It was such a relief to find somebody who sided with us.

After half term, Stuart struggled and was getting breathless, but he was still happy and contented and not in any pain. We talked a lot about how he was feeling. By this stage, he was being given a small dose of morphine which lifted his spirits and let him be more active. We bought a table tennis table for the back garden which gave him loads of pleasure. With the practice he got from Peter, he became quite good.

Peter and I started to concentrate more on our time left with Stuart. We closed in as a family unit and did not particularly want to share him with others. It must be hard for people to imagine, your first-born son, beginning to deteriorate before your very eyes. He still responded in the normal ways as a loving child, but he was visibly beginning to slow and lose the action associated with a developing, growing boy. A sense of dread filled us as parents as we saw, in front of us, the same child who we'd brought up, and who was such an integral part of the family, fading away.

Our love as a family and for our children was intensified, as can be imagined. The impending fate awaiting us bound us more tightly together. Despite the cruel treatments that were inflicted on Stuart, he managed to offer us such joy and hope. This is the son, who for thirteen years had developed from a cute baby into an active and vibrant child with an enquiring and agile mind, always having an enthusiastic sense of fun. He was ever adventurous, and we used to wonder how he was frightened of so little.

As a small child, Stuart was undaunted by new experiences and seemed to take most things easily in his stride. Going to nursery school and then onto junior school, joining the Wakefield swimming club, speeding skilfully along on his bike, joining the Sea Cadets, moving to a new house and changing schools as Peter's job moved us around the country. He acted as, what we amusingly called, a 'pathfinder' to his sister and brother, always leading them off into new adventures. This wonderful child was the boy heading for a critical tragedy and, as parents, it was a heavy, demanding burden to bear. It was hard to think of such an innocent young boy who we'd guided through all the years of his early life and who was about to leave the family forever. We were racked with emotional pain that seemed to seat itself somewhere in the lower chest or just a bodily ache, giving a persistent nagging, worrying feeling. At our most anguished moments, at points near despair, all we had to do was to be with Stuart, and somehow our spirits always lifted.

December was approaching and it was obvious to us that Stuart's time was limited. I understood the reasoning behind the hospital's policy of facing up to death, as many people might be in ignorance of their prognosis or worrying about the process of dying. But I knew that children cope well in these situations, better than adults. I still believe, that for our family, we made the right decision not to force Stuart into confronting the fact that his life would end in a few weeks. Our approach might not have been right for other families or someone of a different age or personality, but it worked for us.

On Tuesday 2nd of December, despite being extremely tired, Stuart wanted to go Christmas shopping with me in Wakefield. It was not particularly easy for him to get about as he was short of breath and energy. He enjoyed the outing as he walked about slowly, and I loved him being with me. I parked near the shopping centre so that he did not have to walk far, and I wandered around the shops with him in a buoyant mood. That was the last time he went out. The next day he was well but tired and he stayed in bed, although he insisted that I went to the school to get his physics homework. It was a test paper, and he completed it in bed. When it was marked, later, he got a hundred per cent.

Then on Thursday, the next day, he did not want to get out of bed, and he refused breakfast. The GP came to visit him and at lunchtime, Dr Boyd, the consultant, and Denise, the senior oncology nurse, from St James's hospital, came to the house. They brought more medication and wanted to put up an intravenous drip. Stuart was not happy with the idea of a drip, so he was given a muscular injection of diamorphine.

I knew we had to somehow tell Bridgette and James that Stuart was dying. It was another harrowing moment in my life. That was extraordinarily hard for them to have the words voiced that their brother was about to die. It was another tough thing that I had to cope with. I wanted to protect all my children, but I could not. I could not protect any of them from what was about to happen. Not Stuart, not Bridgette, nor James or Peter for that matter. I knew this would be the last time our three children would be together, and it left me heartbroken and numb. The nurse in me was telling me to keep strong, for just a little bit longer.

That evening Stuart watched a bit of television until about eight. Bridgette and James, before they went to bed, put his Christmas presents on the end of his bed and kissed him goodnight. Stuart by then was lapsing into semi-consciousness. We let him rest and he just lay there, catching his breath but not in any pain. One of us stayed with him. It was obvious that he knew we were there, as he would try and smile from time to time.

As it got later into the evening, we could see Stuart's breathing was difficult, but the medication kept him restful. We could see his breathing becoming shallower and shallower. As he lay there running out of breath, we told him we loved him, and we got a faint response that was like saying goodbye.

When I was nursing, I saw many people die, but I don't think I ever saw anyone die in such a contented, relaxed way as Stuart did. We were all in the house with him. There was no jamboree, no doctors, no nurses, or anyone to interfere with what was the anguished parting and the splitting of our family.

After his breathing stopped, Peter and I sat quietly watching him. Feeling too much pain to cry, we stared at him for a long time as he looked so peaceful. His skin was still full of life and his eyes were shut, just like he was asleep. There was nothing to disturb us as we quietly tried to take in what had just happened. Mixed with the tragedy, it was a cherished moment looking down at our beautiful son. Such an experience changes you forever, as there is always a lingering sense of deep sadness that never leaves you. Bridgette and James were still awake and came in to say their final farewell to Stuart. We were all changed people, who will never forget and will always have this sadness. Stuart died silently in his bed with Peter and me at his bedside at 11:30 in the evening on Thursday 4 December 1986.

Chapter 9

Our children are the most important things in our lives and our love is unconditional. Our future with this most precious boy was gone. Our future felt empty. Bridgette and James's futures were changed. This was not how we had predicted the blossoming of our family. Somehow, we had to learn to bear the tragedy and the feeling of being isolated in our grief.

We all had our separate ways of coping with that heart-breaking night. Having been able to do it on so many occasions during Stuart's illness, I was able to play act. I had learnt to distance myself from my innermost desperate feelings when I saw my family suffering. I desperately wanted to ease their pain. Whenever I hear the song "The Great Pretender", it reminds me of the misery of trying to cover up my grief. My nursing training taught me how to bottle up my emotions, or perhaps I learnt it at boarding school, or I learnt it during the first six months of my life in the children's home. My mother said that when she collected me, at six months old, I could not smile.

I discovered that I needed to talk about Stuart to anyone who would listen. Peter found it hard to even mention Stuart's name without breaking down, and that is the same for him to this day. We talk about Stuart often, but it always brings a tear to Peter's eye.

Bridgette, who was then twelve, stayed in our bed for three days and just wept solidly. She understood precisely what had happened and she felt such loss for her big brother who had always been like a guiding light. James aged ten, found it particularly bewildering and he just wanted to go to school as normal and to try and push the grief out of his mind. He hated feeling sad. None of our ways of coping was either right or wrong. We were individuals within a fractured family unit, managing the best way we could.

What was cruel was that we have no family photographs of Stuart's last Christmas since our camera had been stolen a year before. It still hurts deeply decades later. Another cruel twist was that the school entered an assignment of Stuart's into a national maths competition. We knew nothing about it until the school told us that he had come first. However, we were told that the award was handed to the next person instead, because Stuart was no longer around to collect the prize. That really hurt.

Peter and I had been warned by the hospital social worker, that parents, after the death of a child, can sometimes find it exceedingly difficult to comfort each other. Some sort of blame can often materialise, which can drive couples apart and, in the worst cases, lead to divorce. It's hard when you are both suffering, one not more than the other, with both having the same sense of loss, manifesting itself in different types of behaviour. As a couple, we felt broken but united in our grief and we came through as strong as ever with never a thought of a separation. Imagine what a terrible legacy it would have been for Stuart if we had parted. How desperate would that have been for Bridgette and James, who in their way had done their best to hold the family together? They had never been selfish in demanding our attention. They had always appeared to sense that Stuart's need was so great, although they did seem to know that they equally had our love.

Today in my head, Stuart is not a thirteen-year-old boy anymore. He has grown older with me. I talk to him most days and know he would have had many wonderful attributes and achieved so much, just as Bridgette and James have done. I'm proud of all my children. I still worry decades later about the effect that Stuart's death has had on Bridgette and James, and wonder if I could have done things differently to make their grief easier.

People's reactions towards us were strange after Stuart died. I don't blame them, as it's difficult for people to understand how to react to the death of a child. Some of his teachers were amazing in their support. Others did not know what to say, being too embarrassed, and some crossed over the road to avoid us. I suppose it was to do with not mentioning Stuart so as not to upset us. The odd friend said, "Don't worry, you can have another child to replace Stuart." How does that work, replacing Stuart? But on balance, saying something is better than saying nothing. It does not matter how it comes out. Just knowing that someone remembers, and cares is enough. We were aware of how difficult it was for our friends and family, especially Peter's parents. They suffered greatly and were heartbroken that one of their grandchildren had died at such a young age. Of course, my parents had both died three years earlier and never knew how much Stuart had suffered. All our friends tried to help in their own way. The Prison Service was particularly good to Peter, giving him whatever time off work he needed.

I suffer from a sense of hurt when people come out with clichés such as "time heals". I would argue that in the circumstances of a child's death, time does not heal. You just learn to live with the pain. One suggestion from somebody came out as, "Was it to do with something you fed him as a baby?" Stuart was breastfed until he was nine months old, so that silly remark can be ruled out. What was supposed to be a comforting phrase, came out as "good always comes out of bad". It would take a huge stretch of the imagination to accept that anything good would develop from my thirteen-year-old son dying. A well-meaning friend tried to empathise by comparing the death of my child to her getting divorced. It was obvious that people were trying to be kind, and often they did not think about what they were saying.

We all know of people or close relatives who die of cancer, and we hear the awful expressions from time to time, about cancer involving some kind of battle. "He won his battle against cancer", or "...our war on cancer", or "he fought cancer so bravely". The implication of all this is that those suffering just need to fight the disease with enough vigour, and in that way, it can somehow be 'beaten'. I wonder how these expressions make people feel when the disease progresses, and they become terminally ill. It's a complicated and intricate illness, where there are so many variations to the disease. Cancer has so many twists and turns involving faulty cell growth. The progression of cancer should never be likened to a battlefield. If winning a battle relies on the depth of endeavour, then when death does occur, is the sufferer seen as being defeated? It's easy to imagine how awful it must be for us as a family to have Stuart regarded as having "lost his battle" because somehow, he did not fight hard enough. People certainly mean well when they talk about a person's battle against cancer, but for me that sort of war correlation is difficult to understand. There are so many more appropriate, softer, kinder words that could be used to describe the suffering of a loved one.

The other expression I hate is "sorry for your loss". We have not lost Stuart. He's not just hiding around the corner. We have not mislaid him. He died. You could say we are lost without him, that is certainly true.

Funnily enough, one thing I could not do for twenty years after Stuart died, was to read a novel. I could only read non-fiction. Novels, however well-written, with their stories of escapism from real life, seemed so meaningless. I could not concentrate on reading what I thought of as trivia. I have now, eventually, found my way back into reading fiction and enjoying all categories of literature.

One way of coping after Stuart died was to immerse myself into organising charity events for the Candlelighters, the children's cancer charity which was, at the time, based at St James's Hospital in Leeds and now at the Leeds General Infirmary. I got a sense of satisfaction from raising money to help research into childhood cancers and funding specialist doctors as well as providing a Leeds hospice for children. But if I'm truthful, my efforts were for selfish reasons, as I was somehow trying to keep Stuart alive.

I kept a diary from the day Stuart was diagnosed, documenting his illness, our family life, his drug regime, and his operations. I started writing the diary knowing that his prognosis was not good, and I did not want to forget any detail of what I guessed might be the last eighteen months of his life. I now know I would not have forgotten even the smallest detail of our wonderful boy's horrible journey. Stuart was loved so deeply.

The pain of grief eats remorselessly at you all the time. It's intense, persistent and debilitating for many years and decades afterwards. My grief is just under the surface, with so many sudden cruel as well as happy moments to recall. At anniversary points like the date of his death, Christmas or his birthday, the sadness returns in full measure. We always try and do something pleasurable on those dates and on anniversaries we take his ashes with us if we go out in the car. Stuart's ashes are on top of the Welsh dresser in our kitchen, waiting to be buried with one of us. At the various family weddings, we publicly acknowledge the missing member of our family. Today we have our wonderful two other children and loving, cuddly, happy, playful grandchildren who dive into our bed in the mornings when they are staying with us. Our oldest grandchild has Stuart as his middle name.

When someone asks the question, "How many children do you have?" my heart sinks. I can't bring myself to say two, so I always say three, then dread any further questions. After Stuart died, I so wished I could have had the support, comfort and strength of a mother. I find myself saying, as you would in the school playground, "It's just not fair." For so many people in the world, life "is just not fair", so what makes us as a family any different?

Stuart was a great fan of Dire Straits. Peter is the family poet and over the years has compiled a folder of poems highlighting major events in the lives of our wider family. Ten years after Stuart died, Peter penned a particular poem which he sent to Mark Knopfler of Dire Straits, wondering if he would be interested in putting it to music. We got a warm letter back saying how touched he was, and how pleased that his music was special to Stuart. However, he said he never worked with other lyricists or songwriters, as he found it difficult to "feel" the music when the words had come from others.

Part 3:

—

Fruitless Search

Chapter 10

This is not a subject our daughter, Bridgette, likes to talk about, but the following account was a huge, near tragic, event in our lives, so close to Stuart's death. It happened, in 1987, the year after Stuart died. Up until that point we had been in no mood to have any sort of vacation. But in August we decided we should take a camping holiday. We packed the car, put our large canvas tent on the roof rack, and headed to Northwest Spain. It was an area we hadn't visited before. We set off armed with maps, a book on campsites and a phrase book.

It turned out not to be the relaxing holiday that we had planned. The first few days were wonderful apart from the twenty-four-hour ferry from Plymouth to Santander, across the Bay of Biscay, as I get seasick. Once on dry land we headed west and ended up at a campsite in the harbour town of Muros. There was a thick low mist, so I don't have much memory of what the place looked like. All the shops had umbrella stands at their entrances, so that should have been a clue to the normal weather conditions.

In the supermarket, I bought a bottle of red wine. But as I picked it off the shelf it dropped out of my hand and smashed onto my foot, slicing through my leather sandal and seriously cutting the base of my left big toe. The mixture of blood and red wine flowing across the aisle floor was embarrassing and at the same time a bit ridiculous as you could not tell which was wine and which was blood. I gave my apologies, in the best way I could, and limped out of the shop leaving a trail of blood along the pavement. On returning to the car, I patched up my toe with butterfly stitches from our first aid kit.

To escape the damp weather, we drove inland for about five hours and found an idyllic campsite near Astorga. We became friendly with the camp owner and his son who ran the only local bar-cum-restaurant. It was hot and after a few days the stream where Bridgette and James had been playing dried up. Then one evening, quite late, while we were still eating in the bar, there was a tremendous wailing to be heard around the village. The bar owner and his son had been found dead at the bottom of a local well. They had climbed into the well to test the water levels, given the extreme drought, and they had died of methane gas poisoning. The whole village and campsite closed down. It was a sad occasion but there was nothing we could do to help so we gave our condolences and moved on.

Next, we headed to the north coast so that we would not be too far from Santander to board our ferry home. We found an attractive campsite by the beach at Vidiago. At last, we could relax and enjoy our holiday. But that was not to be. Bridgette and James were strong club swimmers. However, Bridgette had broken her leg in a gym class at school some eight weeks previously and was just getting her strength back after it had been in a plaster cast for six weeks. Bridgette was twelve and James eleven.

They were playing in the waves close to where Peter and I were lying on the beach. Suddenly James came running to us saying that Bridgette had disappeared in the waves, and he could not find her. Peter, instantly, ran out into the sea to search for her. That left me and James on the beach to raise the alarm. I could not speak Spanish and there were no British people on the beach. What I had learnt from our stay near Astorga was in an emergency the Spanish wail and cry, so I did the same as loud as I could. This did not come naturally but it got the whole beach's attention. I pointed out to sea and the message was soon picked up by everybody. By this time not only Bridgette had disappeared but also Peter.

When standing on the beach, with James, my whole body was frozen in despair. I stood there full of hopelessness and anguish. The strong temptation to run into the sea after Peter was overwhelming. That would not have been a practical thing to have done. I needed to raise the alarm and be with James who could sense how dangerous the situation had become. I had to push the thought out of my mind about what would happen if Bridgette and Peter did not reappear on the beach. I tried to stay positive, desperately believing that this tragedy could not be unfolding in front of my eyes.

I soon discovered that most of the young Spaniards on the crowded beach could not swim. But suddenly from the back of the sloping beach came our saviour. A young man dashed down the beach, tipped a woman off her air bed and then used it as a raft to paddle out into the sea. Peter was swimming, beyond the breakers about a hundred metres out into the bay, when suddenly he saw two heads. With some relief, he thought someone was saving Bridgette. As the Spaniard reached Peter he signalled to where he could see Bridgette and another person about ten metres away from him. They were now some hundred and fifty metres from the beach. The Spaniard got to them first on his inflatable and dragged out of the water a young boy clinging to Bridgette. Bridgette later told us that she was on the verge of drowning. She was completely exhausted, a feeling of peace had overwhelmed her and thoughts of her brother

Stuart came into her head. Both children were then draped across the air bed and Peter and the Spaniard brought Bridgette and the boy back to safety.

What had happened was that Bridgette had been happily jumping around in the waves near the shoreline when she was grabbed from below. Someone was wrapping themselves around her legs and then climbing up her body and tightly pinning her arms to her side. Bridgette was powerless to get her arms free to try and help. The person was a twelve-year-old boy, the same age as Bridgette, who could not swim and found himself drowning. Bridgette tried her best to save him, but the current was strong, and he was in a terrifying panic, clinging to her like a limpet. He was climbing up her body trying to save himself as they were both being carried out to sea. All the time Bridgette was trying to keep the two of them buoyant, but her energy was draining.

Between James's quick alert, Peter swimming out into the sea, my wailing, and the Spaniard from the beach, we managed to save the most unthinkable disaster. Peter's instinct to get into the water and to somehow know where to swim even though he could not see Bridgette over the height of the waves saved her life.

The whole episode lasted about twenty minutes. The boy was in a worse state than Bridgette. When they were safely back on the beach, it was obvious that they had both swallowed a lot of seawater. I went with Bridgette and the boy to the local surgery to have them checked out by a doctor. The boy's parents were not on the beach. We did not know where they were. Thankfully, all turned out well in the end, much to our relief. Bridgette was hailed a hero by the camp owner and the boy's family. To her great embarrassment, she was presented with many gifts. After a day's recovery, we headed home. I was never so pleased to land back on British soil. How could my daughter have vanished and my husband too, especially after Stuart had died the previous year? It was so close.

After we arrived home, it became increasingly important for me to recognise the connection between the three events. My eldest son had died, my adoptive mother could not conceive children, and my birth mother had 'lost' what I presumed to be her eldest child. I saw a pattern here and I was afraid this was the strange destiny of the women in my family. I needed to break this insidious cycle. Of course, I could do nothing about myself or my adoptive mother, but my birth mother could get her daughter back. This would thwart fate and prevent our daughter from running into the same pain we had all suffered. I know this sounds silly, but it was the way I felt at the time, and it's difficult to articulate these superstitious emotions to others. My birth mother getting her daughter back was, of course, dependent on her still being alive, and whether I was able to find her. The serious search began.

At the start of my search came the question from everyone I knew: "Why do you want to search?" Endless books and articles have been written about this, and they all ask the question why do it, particularly when you are likely to offend someone along the way? I explain to myself that I have spent my life feeling guilty about other people's secrets, so why should I not search and confront those secrets to find the truth for myself? I feared that some might see this as being selfish. My adoptive parents were now dead, but I did sense they would have supported my journey to find my birth mother. Even though we never discussed it, I knew they suspected that one day, it was likely to happen.

Friends and family, and even strangers, would often question my motives telling me that I was being disloyal to my adoptive parents who had cared for me since being a baby. Telling them that I'm searching because "I just wanted to, I'm curious and it's a mystery", or "I was saving my daughter from some hidden future agony", did not seem to be the answer that people wanted to hear. Or, what I thought they wanted to hear. People expected to get an answer, along the lines that I needed to find out about my family's medical history for my children's sake. And some wanted me to say that I had a compulsion to find my roots and family lineage.

In a confused way, half of me found it exciting to think that I could journey through life with a clean ancestry slate. On the other hand, I wanted a genetic line to hand down to my children. I can't deny that I was stimulated by the prospect of a thrilling journey of discovery in unearthing my birth origins. Although, nagging cautions and concern for other people's feelings, held me back. I had to decide whether to remain ignorant or go down the path of exploring the circumstances of my birth.

I was becoming aware that searching for my birth mother involves much more than "filling in the gaps on a family history chart". Coming to terms with the emotional side of my birth I found confusing and less easy to confront. The ever-powerful question always kept repeating, as to why I should be excluded from knowing my past. The answer to that question is, that I should not be excluded. Why should my heritage be the preserve of the adoption bureaucracy? It's not down to an organisation to stand guard over my birth details because that information is my birthright. I'm a grown-up, I did not feel I needed protection. But perhaps my birth mother does. Then why should I continually bear her guilt? Surely it can now be healed.

Adoption is a good thing, and adoptive parents should be applauded. I have a lot for which to be thankful. However, I recognise that adoption clearly can be a challenging situation for all concerned. So much secrecy surrounds the entire process for the child, birth mother and adoptive parents. I find it difficult to allow myself to reflect on my emotions. It's frustrating not to be able to explain to myself, let alone to others, the trauma of rejection and separation, even though it was at birth. It must be so much harder for an older child. I'm sure I will say this more than once, but I'm eternally grateful to my adoptive parents for the life they gave me, the sacrifices they made and for moulding me into the balanced person I am today. They taught me the skills to cope with whatever life throws at me.

Following Stuart's death and Bridgette's near drowning, the intensity of the feeling of "just wanting to know my origins" became overwhelming. I never really welcomed the question of why search, but always hoped for acceptance from my family and friends, which I just did. The issues of belonging and nurture versus nature became intriguing to me. It would be inevitable that my views in this area were likely to change over time.

Until 1990, all the information I had was my original birth certificate with my mother's name. I had discovered I was born in Bramshott, Hampshire on 11 September 1945 in a Canadian military base field hospital. I knew my mother was in the Canadian forces as a clerk and her home address was in Edmonton, Alberta, Canada. By 26 September 1945, shortly after my birth, she had moved to Alderbrook Park to recuperate, without me. At this point, I had been placed with the National Children Adoption Association at 71 Knightsbridge, London. When I walk down Knightsbridge and see number 71, I imagine that somewhere in that building was me, as a tiny, unsmiling, underweight, lonely baby, with the name Donna Mary Hamilton.

I had already written to Knightsbridge in 1978 and their reply, after looking in their records, told me that my mother was in the Canadian forces and that most of the arrangements for my adoption had been through a social worker attached to the

Canadian Air Force. The Agency had confirmed that they had no further information. I already had my mother's name, her address and the home where I had been placed. I thought this was all the information that I needed and that my search, from here on, was going to be easy. How wrong could I be?

Chapter 11

My serious search began in early 1990. I joined NORCAP, the National Organisation for the Counselling of Adoptees and Parents, based in Oxford. Not because I needed counselling, but because they had produced an informative booklet called "Searching for Family Connections". I found this useful to a point, but it only covered the UK, while my search was likely to take me to Canada. However, I did write to all the establishments suggested in the booklet, just in case my mother had left a trail behind in England. I entered my details in a search register where, if there had been any inquiry made by my mother or any other birth relative, we would be automatically matched.

I was excited and optimistic. I went to the local library and wrote to every organisation that I could find listed under anything to do with adoption or missing persons. These included The Surrey Record Office, The Hampshire Record Office, and an RAF (Royal Air Force) research specialist, at the National Archives at Kew in Richmond near London, called Alice. Also, the Salvation Army, the Catholic Welfare Society and so the list went on. I included my name on another national register that was set up by The Department of Health, as an adoption contact point, following the 1989 Children Act.

Most of my enquiries drew a blank but all replied with sympathetic letters, trying to make suggestions as to a way forward. The NORCAP magazine encouraged adoptees to write letters explaining their search and why they were searching. The magazine printed these letters under the heading of "Reunion Stories" or "Still Searching". I wrote a letter to NORCAP, explaining my feelings about being adopted and saying that I had had no luck with my search. I got to the point of thinking it was unlikely that I would ever find my birth mother, given that she was Canadian. I received some wonderfully warm, heart-rending letters from people in situations like mine. The only difference is that they were all offspring of UK birth parents.

At NORCAP's suggestion, I sent a lengthy article to them titled, "Is There Ever a Greener Grass?". The substance of the article was that I classed myself as having been lucky to have been adopted. I was grateful to my birth mother for having made the terrible decision to give me away shortly after I was born. I described all the thoughts that had been going around my head, related to the circumstances of my search. I finished with the suggestion that it would be wonderful to find my mother, if for no other reason than to say that I was well and that I would like to thank her for making that difficult decision all those years ago. NORCAP published the article in full.

NORCAP was set up in 1982, and it held the first register, in the UK, to link adopted people with birth relatives. After January 2013 it closed, mainly because its job was done. They were instrumental in changing the law in the UK to give people over the age of eighteen, the automatic entitlement to their birth records. Many other agencies have now taken over the work of NORCAP, but the contact register is still available through Family Action.

Having been conceived during the Second World War by an unmarried mother, I consider that I have come out of everything quite well, given the circumstances. My birth mother, on the other hand, found herself alone in a foreign country, giving birth to a baby, who she knew she could never take home to Canada. I was sure she was likely to carry the shame and guilt of what happened in England for the rest of her life.

I was starting to get despondent with my search, as every angle I pursued turned into a dead end. It was not going to be as straightforward as I had once hoped. The issue for me was that, once I had started my search, I could not give up. It was like a puzzle that had to be solved, and I found it impossible to stop, even though I seemed not much further forward than when I started. The emotional drive of wanting to obtain my birth records grew stronger with every setback.

To get anywhere, I realised I needed to widen my search into Canada, a country I knew nothing about and hadn't visited. In June 1990, I wrote to the Canadian High Commission in London. The Commission replied saying that they did not provide a tracing service, and I should try my local Red Cross. They suggested that the Red Cross would send a questionnaire for me to complete. This form would then be sent to the National Red Cross, who would forward it to their headquarters in Geneva, who would then send it to the relevant branch office in Canada. However, the Red Cross were not interested in my story, as they did not see it as any kind of emergency, nor a compelling enough case to call for a search on compassionate grounds.

So when I got the reply from the Red Cross, I felt immensely guilty for wasting their time. It did discourage me from carrying on and I was prompted to rethink what I was doing. I asked myself whether I was being selfish and self-indulgent when there were far more pressing problems in the world. My confidence was knocked by the thought that people had to reply to my insignificant requests.

After years of mulling over the question of whether I should be searching, doubts about the appropriateness of what I was doing were beginning to sneak into my head. However, I concluded that I could not stop, I had become addicted to the search and had to continue.

My search so far had brought me to April 1991, and I had spent months writing even more letters, but with little success. I wrote to the British High Commission in Ottawa asking for advice, but that proved to be useless. They gave me two addresses, one with a Canadian adoption register and the other to The Triad Society for Truth in Adoption of Canada. Neither of these organisations responded to my letters with any interest because I had been born outside Canada. Yet, I had been born on Canadian soil in a wartime Canadian services field hospital. I was suffering from the view that I was being shunted from one organisation to another, and no one was interested in helping me.

The limited information I got from Knightsbridge was depressing. I was told that because I was born on a Canadian Forces Base, none of my records would be stored in England. Any further details would have gone back to Canada and would be filed amongst my mother's Canadian Air Force records. Also, I was born before the National Health Service was properly formed and my English birth records would have been patchy at best or perhaps not have survived at all.

The firm piece of evidence I had was that my mother was from Edmonton, Alberta. This seemed a good place to start to further my research. I found an organisation in her home city called Parent Finders. Parent Finders of Canada is part of a national network which originated in Vancouver in 1976. It was set up to help reunite family members separated by adoption or those who had been fostered. I paid thirty dollars to join their register to find out if there was a match with my biological mother. I was not convinced that my birth mother would ever have accessed this register let alone added her name to it, and unfortunately, the trail with Parent Finders went dead, even though I had renewed my annual subscription to their magazine.

My next step was to write to the Base Commander of Air Command at the Canadian Forces Base in Winnipeg. Again, I was not hopeful of a result as half a million Canadians, mostly young single men, had been posted to Britain for lengthy periods between 1939 and 1946. My letter got passed on to a research assistant who forwarded my letter to the Personnel Records Centre at the National Archives of Canada in Ottawa. An unhelpful letter came back saying that they could not help me, because a review of my mother's service documents revealed that she hadn't accessed her records in over forty-five years. I could not understand why that meant I was not allowed to have access to her records. They also said that the address she gave during her service period was no longer valid and that they could not find her. I took their reply at face value and became further despondent, thinking it may not be possible to trace her at all. Then I learnt that war records in Canada were protected by vast amounts of red tape and an impregnable Privacy Act.

A year after first contacting Canada, it was still challenging to get any information. I was told that I could only access my mother's records if she gave me permission. As I barely knew who she was, let alone where she lived, that hurdle seemed insurmountable. It was frustrating to think that Canadian veterans and their families had their privacy so protected that an abandoned baby from the war could not pursue their parentage. Compared to the rights of Canadian service personnel, the rights of a child born out of wedlock to a Canadian carried no weight at all. This was manifestly unfair. To complicate matters even further, I learnt that I would have been allowed to see my mother's service records if she had died during the war. I knew, of course, that my mother did not die and was very much alive at the end of the war when she gave birth to me. Being told I was not a Canadian citizen made it even more complicated.

I had to become more ingenious if this search was to be successful. I sent for a copy of the 1985 Canadian Privacy Act. It was a hefty 27-page document duplicated in French. Its purpose was to "...protect the privacy of individuals with respect to personal information about themselves". I read the document carefully, highlighting areas that I thought might give me grounds for appeal or complaint against the Act. However, without legal help, which I could not afford, I was unlikely to construct any kind of case that would carry weight.

Whilst I was occupied with the Canadian connection, I had come across some publicity about a group in the Walsall area, near Birmingham, England, called War Babies. The group was originally set up for people to trace US servicemen, who had romantic liaisons with British women during the Second World War, resulting in them becoming fathers.

War Babies set itself the task of trying to trace these absent fathers, and the group had met with some success. I was unusual in that I had a Canadian mother. Given the vast number of liaisons between English girls and foreign troops, there was a popular catchphrase about the North American servicemen that said, "over-paid, over-sexed and over here".

I found Sandra, the woman who had set up War Babies, to be pleasant and helpful. She organised a mini conference at the Savoy Hotel in Blackpool. This was for the War Babies group to meet over a weekend to discuss adoption and search issues. The group had widened its activities to include Canadian servicemen. Peter and I decided to go along and see whether it could offer any help. It might give me a different avenue to pursue.

I joined the group, paid my fee, which from memory was around £30, and booked into the large hotel on the Blackpool seafront. Sandra was good at getting publicity for the group and had arranged for a few of us to have telephone interviews with the Globe and Mail, Canada's national newspaper. Because my case appeared interesting, she organised that I would be filmed, at my home in Wakefield, for a news item on Canadian Television Network (CTN). These interviews were done in advance of our Savoy Hotel meeting, ready to go out in Canada on the day of the War Babies get-together.

Peter and I drove to Blackpool from Wakefield. I remember the weekend vividly. It was 23 November 1991. As we walked into the Savoy Hotel that Saturday evening, there was a group of about eight people, collected in a far corner of the lounge. They were visibly upset, with one crying. I was sure they must be part of the War Babies group. I was worried that this was going to be the depressing theme for the evening meeting, which was to be held over dinner. Most of the group from War Babies had booked into the hotel overnight. I was not feeling sad or downhearted, but quite the opposite. I was optimistic and looked forward to hearing about other people's searches.

Having seen the downcast gathering in the corner, Peter and I booked in and went straight to our room. We went for a walk along the promenade in the cold windy November evening. Our room, in this late Victorian building, was facing the sea along with about a hundred and forty other rooms that overlooked the beach. Before the meeting, I must admit we discussed whether we should "do a runner" and forget the whole thing. But we had paid for our room and dinner, and so decided to see it through.

In the early evening, about thirty of us gathered for a buffet meal in one of the hotel's private rooms. There was a mixture of those searching for either their US or Canadian fathers, not their mothers. This did make me feel a little isolated as my search was quite different from those present. Small groups of people sat at individual tables with a number who already knew each other. We sat with a pleasant, easy-going couple who, like us, were new to War Babies.

After we had eaten, Sandra gave a brief presentation on the work she had done to help people acquire various adoption papers. Her delivery was a bit stilted, and she was not polished at getting her message across. However, the whole idea of the event was for us to mix and swap notes so that we could learn from other people's experiences. In fairness, I was not expecting a slick performance. As it turned out we only spoke to the couple at our table, whose history was nothing like mine. After we had swapped stories, we ended up having a general chit-chat.

Suddenly there was a bit of a commotion in the room when one person started loudly accusing Sandra of taking our fees and not being accountable as to what she had done with the money. Sandra was put in an embarrassing position. Her husband tried to explain how the money from the joining fee had been used. It all became heated, with some people being rude and challenging towards poor Sandra. The group did have a Secretary and Treasurer, but they did not come to her help. Being so new to the group, it was difficult for me to judge the situation. As far as I was concerned, Sandra had got me a Canadian television interview and an article in the Globe and Mail, so I thought she had done a decent job.

Sandra had explained to me in an earlier letter that her quarterly telephone bill was a few hundred pounds and that on average, she spent nine pounds a week on postage. Her heart was in the right place, and she seemed as though she genuinely wanted to help people. She had launched the group after helping her husband trace his father's GI family in the US. From what I could work out concerning the administration fees she charged, she hardly made a fortune. Accusing her of running a money-making operation seemed misplaced. Bizarrely, with all the acrimony and shouting, the evening was quite entertaining. With our companions, we sat back and watched the "floor show". As can be imagined, my aim of trying to move the search forward was not advanced by the Blackpool event. What the weekend in Blackpool did, however, was rekindle my desire to keep searching, so I was grateful to Sandra, despite what turned out to be an odd experience.

On the following day on the way home, we heard on the car radio that Freddie Mercury, from the rock group Queen, had died at the age of 45. I was a great fan of Queen and was saddened to hear of his death. I had known that he had been ill for a while with AIDS, but was not expecting his sudden demise. We drove home listening to the radio playing Queen songs as a tribute to the singer. The songs made me feel downhearted and tearful as Stuart was also a fan of Queen. Friends had taken him, a few months before he died, to see a live Queen concert in Newcastle. He was ecstatic and it gave him such a "buzz". He loved every minute of the concert as it made him, for a short while, forget about his cancer. At the time I had been so worried as he was out of my sight for a few hours. I was very protective of Stuart.

Chapter 12

I wrote again to the National Adoption Association, located in Knightsbridge, London, who had organised my adoption. I don't know why I did this as I had drawn a blank with them earlier. But surprise surprise, I got a letter back from the City of Westminster's Department of Social Services. They held all the files, as the adoption agency in Knightsbridge was now closed. Earlier the Agency had told me that there were no files available. Now they were saying something different. They said they were "…unable to deal directly with adopted people unless they have been referred directly to us by the General Register Office". This office, for England, held all the records of births, deaths and marriages. They also said it was their policy only to send the file of an adopted person to his or her appointed counsellor. It felt as if I was aboard the old merry-go-round again. I had to go through a counsellor to be judged of sound mind. My view was that the records of my adoption were my property and jumping through other people's hoops was not appropriate.

Once again, I felt angry and marginalised, as I was officially told, at the age of forty-six, that I needed the services of a counsellor before I could have my birth details. If I had been asked if I might like to consider going through a counsellor, I would have found that more reasonable. I sent a letter to the Social Services Department in my hometown of Wakefield, explaining the situation to them.

Whilst I was waiting for the reply from Wakefield, I decided I needed to have a multi-pronged approach to my search. I needed to be more inventive and think the whole thing through more laterally. I researched the RCAF (Royal Canadian Air Force) and developed an interest in Bomber Command during the Second World War, which got me searching libraries and second-hand book shops for information.

I sent another letter to the National Archives of Canada in Ottawa and got much the same reply as before, saying, amongst other things, that they could not, or would not, release any information on my mother. At this point, I did not know whether she was alive or dead. However, what they did in their response, was to enclose her dates of entry and departure from the RCAF. Now I knew the date of her enlistment in May 1943 in Edmonton, Alberta, as well as the date of her discharge in August 1946 in Winnipeg, Manitoba. A tiny bit more of the jigsaw slipped into place. Even though I still lacked much hard detail, it did, however, make me feel I was making some progress.

I wrote to different Air Force and Legion magazines both in Britain and Canada. I created slightly vague adverts to be placed in the magazines, suggesting that a person in England was searching for a wartime friend in Canada. These adverts were designed to be targeted specifically at my mother so that no one else would be able to deduce it was her daughter who had written the advertisement. At the same time, just as a means of piecing snippets of information together, I looked up shipping lists to try and find out at which port in Britain my mother might have disembarked. However, I made no headway on this and drew a blank. I hoped my adverts might produce a better result.

Following the correspondence from Ottawa, I wrote them a letter of complaint. My letter highlighted what I thought might be small loopholes in their response to me, based on their interpretation of the Canadian Privacy Act. I listed four specific grounds where I thought they may be at fault in their reply to me. I had little confidence it would get far, and as was to be expected, it did not. But it did make me realise how rigid and inflexible the Canadian Privacy Act was.

I thought that someone, somewhere in the bureaucratic system in Canada, might just warm to my plight. It turned out in the end to be a man called Brian White in the Personnel Records Centre at the National Archives in Ottawa with whom I had been communicating. In my next correspondence, I deliberately changed from using a formal line to a chatty, friendly tone. My earlier formal letters hadn't worked. All the time I was pushing him to give me information and each time he would send back the same official reply, that he could not help. I softened the tone and tried to be cheerful, to see if I could evoke a bit of his empathy. I made the letters a little more amusing. Below, is a transcript of one of the letters I sent in March 1992:

Dear Mr White

Re: Elizabeth Jane Hamilton

It is your favourite correspondent from England again; how are you? Thank you for your letter dated 6 March 1992 in response to my earlier letter posing a few questions. I did note that comparing your letter of December 1991 with your latest, you seem to have been promoted, now being Head of Correspondence and Research – many congratulations.

I have just been assessing my failure rate about questions asked and answers received. From correspondence in August 1990, December 1991 and March 1992, I have asked 15 questions and received two answers: pretty dismal. Downhearted, yes, giving in, no. You have always replied to me which is encouraging.

The key question is whether my mother is alive or dead. I know you can't answer that, so can I put it another way? When I next visit Canada, can you tell me whether I get from the florist a wreath or a greetings bouquet? Maybe that is too direct. Let me try again. If she is dead, can you reply to me by just acknowledging that you have received my letter and say nothing else? If she is alive, can you say you are not allowed to tell me?

I look forward to your reply. In England, having written to me a few times before, it's normal to drop the "madam" and be a little less formal. The use of "madam" is something you might call the Queen.

If you think I'm being obsessive, I do have a calm reason for wanting to try and find my mother and that is contained in the attached letter I wrote to an adoption search organisation in England.

Yours sincerely

A response arrived from Brian White, it was more than just an acknowledgement, calling me by my Christian name and saying that he had put all my correspondence and responses in my mother's file. He also said that if he became aware of my mother's whereabouts, he would inform her of my enquiry. That was about as good as it was going to get from Brian's department but I thought I had at least made some progress.

Brian had also enclosed a list of my mother's RCAF postings. I was grateful for anything that gave me an insight into my mother's movements from when she joined up. I studied every detail of the document, trying to work out all the abbreviations that showed where she had been stationed. Such tiny things were so important to me. It made me feel I was getting nearer to my mother. In reality, of course, I was not that much closer to finding her. Brian knew I was still a long way off from finding her, but I did warm to him. However, he had written a longish reply with some specific details suggesting that reading between the lines, he was telling me that my mother was not dead and that she was still alive. This was considerable progress. I wish I had met Brian in person.

I had, over the months, been in correspondence with the researcher, Alice, at the British National Archives at Kew in London. She was helpful and tried to steer me in the right direction as to how I could further my search. I had a suspicion that she did not believe that adoptive children should search for their birth parents. Despite that, she seemed prepared to find out any information she could about Canadian activities during the war. I sent her my mother's RCAF posting sheet that Brian had sent from Ottawa. This helped to give the search a bit of focus. Alice deduced that when my mother would have arrived in Britain in July 1944, she would have been sent to 3PRC, which was the Canadian Personnel Reception Centre in Bournemouth. I contemplated whether this could raise another line of investigation. Unfortunately, it was not clear which boat she had travelled on from Halifax in Canada, or where she would have disembarked in Britain.

On 11 March 1992, after having written to the Wakefield Social Services Department, I received a letter telling me that they were now in possession of all my papers from Westminster Social Services. Westminster were the custodians of the former National Adoption Association records. In the letter, they said that they had set up an appointment for me to view my documents.

Unfortunately, on the day of the meeting, I was in Barcelona leading a group of textile students from Huddersfield University. By this time, I had changed careers and taken on a full-time job as a lecturer at the University running the BSc Textile Design course. Thankfully, someone from the Adoption Office at the District Council in Wakefield, called John Wood, was extremely sensible. The original idea was to view the papers in John's office and then they would be sent back to Westminster Social Services. It made me question why they could be bothered letting me see these original documents, only for them to be sent back from where they came from. I wondered why they could not just send me copies and be done with it. Seeing that I was going to be away, John managed to obtain permission from Westminster to have the file copied, which he would then put in the post for me. All that seemed a lot more reasonable.

I arrived home from Barcelona at about two in the morning, with a fellow lecturer and friend, Liz. She was staying with us, as she was unable to travel back to her home, given it was well after midnight. We went into the house quietly, as we knew Peter and the children were likely to be asleep. There on the kitchen table was the unopened packet from John. Liz knew all about my search and she was as excited as I was to see it there on the table. We looked at each other with the same question, as to whether we went to bed and abandoned the package until the morning or whether we should open it there and then.

Chapter 13

L iz and I were tired, but a decision had to be made. The decision was whether we should open the brown A4 envelope sitting on the solid old pine kitchen table. It could hold a clue to my roots. Conversely, should it be left until later the next day when I might find time to open it quietly on my own? I had waited a long time for this moment.

I could not resist the temptation and having Liz with me was a good thing because she could keep me grounded when the envelope was opened. How could we go to sleep and leave it sealed until the morning? The excitement and surge of adrenaline made me wide awake. It became obvious that I could not wait until morning when the house would be busy with the children and breakfast.

I opened the packet and read the attached letter from John Wood, the Adoptions Officer at the Social Services Department in Wakefield. The letter said that he was pleased to be able to send me a copy of the file. The original had now been returned to Westminster. His tone appeared apologetic and there was a hint that he may have been a bit disappointed that the file did not have more information.

This was not a good start. I felt a sudden loss of optimism with a sense of "here we go again". I might only get snippets of information, but to me, having some extra scant details about my birth mother would be a bonus. I was getting used to moving ahead at a snail's pace. Any material that I could latch onto would be appreciated, however small. In the packet were twelve pages of various letters, forms completed by my birth mother, a medical questionnaire and a certificate releasing my mother from the RCAF dated 23 August 1946. To get twelve whole pages about myself and my birth mother, though, seemed a breakthrough.

Strangely enough, I did not feel particularly emotional. Excited, yes, but I felt detached with a sense that the documents were fictitious and not about me. I was eager to analyse them, but I was quite calm about the detail unfolding in front of me. The search had been a bumpy ride, it was an adventure, a research project and a problem that had to be solved. I can't explain why I was emotionally dispassionate. I was just too tired.

I had learnt to control my feelings in front of others when Stuart was ill and dying. After Stuart's death, I had taken on more responsibility at Huddersfield University, and I was still selling some of my textile designs. I was juggling my family and work, enabling me not to dwell on what was the immense sadness of Stuart having died. The heartache was so powerful that I could not allow it to surface. I was well-practised at this, as sentimentality and emotional outbursts were not on my parents' agenda. I was raised to be unemotional and was never fussed over as a child.

Being given detailed information on my birth mother was a lot to take in after half a century of not knowing. Could these forms be about the woman who gave birth to me and revealed facts about me as a baby? It was slightly surreal.

Liz and I quickly flicked through the pages as it was too late to read and digest all the information given on the forms that were in front of us. The one thing that seemed to jump off the page, was the statement that my mother was Irish. I was not prepared for that. I was genuinely surprised that I had Irish roots, and I wondered what the explanation was. My mother's address, on my original birth certificate, was Edmonton, Alberta in Canada. At that point Liz and I both burst out laughing with Liz saying, "...so you thought you were Canadian and all along you are Irish." That was the cue to go to bed as we were exhausted and had entered the giggly stage of tiredness. My mind no longer could absorb all the particulars given on these papers that were so significant to me.

As I got into bed next to Peter, I could not help but give him a nudge and whisper in his ear, telling him I was Irish. I got a mumbled response of "What" before he went back to sleep. There was one thing about my husband, in that I could do a jig, an Irish jig, on top of the bed, because once he was asleep, he would never stir. I was sure he hadn't taken in what I had said.

As I was trying to get to sleep, thoughts about my mother's address, Edmonton, Alberta, were spinning around in my mind. I knew that many Irish people emigrated to Canada during the mid-nineteenth century due to the Great Famine of Ireland. So, in some respects, it did make sense that the family could have come from Ireland. The Great Famine was caused by a catastrophic failure of the potato crops. During that period, however, my mother would not have been alive, so that ruled out one explanation for her departure from Ireland.

On the form from Westminster, my mother did not refer to herself as being British but Irish, which begged the question from which side of the border did she come? At this point, I did not know where my mother's family lived in Ireland, and neither did I have any idea when she may have left for Canada. I did not even know whether she was still alive and living in Canada. Although the way Brian White, from the Canadian archives, had answered my letter, it gave me a clue that she was not dead.

As I was trying to fall asleep, I was thinking about when I had qualified as a new State Registered Nurse in 1966. There had been a scheme to try and get British nurses to work in various Commonwealth countries. The thought of emigrating to a place like Canada was intriguing. After the Second World War, the ten-pound, one-way ticket, under the assisted passage scheme offered by Australia and New Zealand, encouraged a lot of people like me to seek a new life abroad. However, the requirement to work for two years and hand over your passport on arrival did not seem so attractive. During the 1960s, Canada, the US and South Africa were amongst other nations that organised financial incentives for British nurses to accept employment in their countries.

The next day was a Saturday and Liz went home. I found a quiet moment to study the contents of the envelope which was still on the kitchen table from the night before. The package included the information given on my birth certificate, so nothing new there. There was also a copy of the application form to The National Children Adoption Society, completed by my birth mother shortly after I was born in 1945. This proved to be much more interesting. She had recorded my status as being illegitimate but said that both she and my birth father were living and healthy. A major piece of information was that she named my father and his nationality as Canadian. That was a stunning surprise. Crucially, at the end of the form she wrote the following words. "We met on the boat coming over to England. We've known each other for about 14 months. We were not engaged. Because I'm not married, I find it impossible to be able to keep the baby." I felt sad for my mother as she must have filled in the form under great duress and anguish. After all, I was not the product of a "one-night stand" by an unknown man. This I found comforting. Although, during wartime that would have been quite understandable. It was clear that there had been a relationship but one that had no future.

Two letters were referencing my mother. The first letter was a confidential report, signed by Captain W.B. Shute, who was the doctor present at my birth. He said in his report describing my mother, "I have known this young lady as a patient for the last three months and have every reason to think that she is a thoroughly respectable girl. I anticipate that she will lead a perfectly satisfactory life in the future and need occasion no worry on that account." The second document was from D. G. Cameron, a squadron welfare officer from the RCAF overseas headquarters, who was based at number 20 Lincoln's Inn Fields, London. She was in charge of my mother's welfare and had organised my adoption. The reference heading was, To Whom It May Concern:

W.312419 Airwoman 1st Class E. Hamilton

The above-named airwoman is a member of the Royal Canadian Air Force (Women's Division) stationed in London. AW1 Hamilton has been overseas for a year and a half, during which time no adverse entry has been made on her Service Conduct Sheet.

The officer for whom she works states that AW1 Hamilton mixes well with her associates and has a pleasant personality. This airwoman is thoroughly reliable in every respect, and her work and demeanour have always been very good.

AW1 Hamilton has borne her unfortunate experience very admirably and feels that in placing her baby with the National Children's Adoption Association, she is taking the only step in assuring her a happy future.

I found it reassuring to know that she had support from the medical team and her head office. It did appear that my mother was an extremely nice, sociable person.

The only other information in the package was a few letters and a date when my adoptive parents came to see me in the adoption home, it was on 19 February 1946. My birth mother signed a form, on 12 June 1946, that said she would be "...deprived of all parental rights and responsibilities". My mother was repatriated to Canada in early July 1946 and was "honourably released" from the RCAF in August. There was a note in my file saying, "Don't write to Miss Hamilton. No one in Canada is aware of the existence of the child Donna Mary."

The Headquarters of the RCAF were keen to expedite the final adoption proceedings, as they were preparing to withdraw their staff from the London office. All my adoptive parents had to do was to turn up and collect me from the home in Knightsbridge. There was a small fee to be paid which I was led to believe was about one shilling, about five pence in today's money. It left two women, one ecstatic and the other heartbroken. The new baby was carried off in the arms of one, whilst the other left the country without her baby, never to see her again. That was a contrast of emotions for two people, but the third person in this equation was me, who inherited a genuine mix-up of feelings.

That was the extent of the information from Westminster. I had to agree with John Wood that I was not a great deal closer to my goal. Yet, I had fragments of fascinating information for which I was grateful. The details filled in a few blanks so that I had a better understanding of the first year of my life. However, on analysing the papers, all that was specifically helpful to my search was the name of my father. But that was a crucial piece of news for me.

At least I now knew that both my parents were alive and well at the time of my birth. I had often wondered whether my father had been killed in the latter part of the war. I would have been conceived around Christmas 1944 or New Year 1945. Victory in Europe (VE) Day, which ended the war in Europe was 8 May 1945. Victory over Japan (VJ) Day is celebrated on 15 August when the Japanese conceded defeat. However, it was not until 2 September 1945 that Japan formally surrendered, bringing the war to a close.

Chapter 14

I made one last further appeal to the Canadian authorities regarding my earlier complaint about their Privacy Act. I received a reply in April 1992 which, as expected, was a non-committal response. They told me, "We must be forthright in our responses ... our offices can't investigate your complaint." I was trying to get any snippet of information from every source possible. I did write again to Brian White at the National Archives in Ottawa, but once more, he told me that without my mother's written consent or proof of her death, I was not entitled to be given any information from her file. I was saddened that Brian's letter confirmed that he had given me as much information as his office would allow.

I decided to do more research into the bits of information I already had about my mother at the time of my birth. By this stage, I knew my place of birth was the Canadian field hospital at Bramshott in Hampshire. I also knew my mother had put her address as Alderbrook Park, near Guildford in Surrey. With nothing much else to go on, it seemed worthwhile to explore these two lines of enquiry. My search felt a bit like a military campaign. I needed to be methodical, keep good notes and pick away at every minuscule detail that came my way.

I received no helpful responses from the various adverts that I had put in the Air Force and Legion magazines. But I did get a letter from a lady, who lived in Kent. She had seen my advert in the magazine. It was a kind note, and she wanted to help. She had cousins in Edmonton, Alberta, who were members of the Canadian Legion. She said she would ask them if they had heard of my mother. This did sound more promising, but sadly, her cousins could not help.

My quest would have been so much easier if the family search site Ancestry had been in existence. Ancestry officially went live online, with the launch of ancestry.com in 1996. But it was not until 2012 that it expanded its business into DNA testing and tracking in the US, and this became available to Britain and Canada in 2015. With my search efforts taking place around 1992, few databases were of any help at that time. I even tried the online family search site of the Latter-Day Saints in Utah. But because I had so little information to feed into the database, it did not throw up a result. I then moved back to the information I had, which was the location of my birth at Bramshott.

We had close friends, Vivienne and Brian, who lived in Hampshire. Peter and I, as well as our son James, went to stay with them in April 1992. James was friendly with Vivienne and Brian's son, as they had been to junior school together. It was a good opportunity to explore the area where I was born. Peter and I visited Bramshott, which is near the A3 road that links London to Portsmouth. Bramshott is where the wartime Canadian Forces General Field Hospital was situated. When we visited the site, it was an empty field, except for some concrete bases where the hospital buildings would have stood. It was quite eerie for me to see the site where I was born, empty but for these concrete plinths half covered by long grass and undergrowth.

However, the Canadians were not forgotten at Bramshott as we found out when we visited the small, attractive 12th-century church of St Mary's which was close to the former hospital. We were surprised to see in the churchyard there were a substantial number of war graves, and 318 graves belonged to First World War Canadian servicemen. The dates on the gravestones were from late 1918 and early 1919. We were mystified, knowing that the war had ended around the Autumn of 1918. We discovered from a leaflet in the church porch that the high number of deaths was not because of conflict but was due to the Spanish Flu pandemic. We also found out later that there were many more Canadians buried in the Roman Catholic Church in the adjoining village of Liphook. It was calculated that around five hundred million people, one-third of the world's population, were infected with the flu virus. The number of actual deaths was thought to have been over fifty million. A truly catastrophic disease.

Inside the church, above the altar, we saw a stained-glass commemorative window that honoured the Canadians who came to Britain to fight in the two world wars. The window shows tiny details of most of the Canadian Provinces. The kneelers in the pews were embroidered with Canadian place names. Many aspects of the church celebrated the memory of the Canadian forces. All this was extremely moving; it gave me a sense of place about the spot where I was born.

I left a note in the church visitors book, giving my contact details. Whilst we were in the church, a volunteer was polishing the pews. He was keen to chat, so we explained why we were visiting. He said he would give my details to the church secretary, and he was sure she would be in touch. Later I received a pleasant letter from the secretary, enclosing a booklet titled, "Canadians" written by Mr Lawrence Giles. She also enclosed a kind letter from Mr

Giles, saying that he was in touch with Mrs Bertha Rudow (née Jones), who had been a Canadian nursing sister in the field hospital from 1944 to 1946. Bertha was a member of the Canadian military, and her home was in Ontario. In Mr Giles's letter, he told me that Bertha pointed out that in 1945, the hospital had opened a small maternity ward for Canadian girls who were "expecting". Bertha had described to him how a Liphook girl cycled to the hospital every day to collect the "baby wash". This was the baby laundry, which impressed the Canadian nursing sisters by always being returned "sparkling fresh". Bertha had sent Mr Giles a photograph of herself holding the winner of the "First Best Baby" competition to be held in Liphook after VE Day. Regrettably, it was not me, it was a local baby.

Mr Giles gave me Bertha's address and encouraged me to write to her. Bertha had worked in a Maternity unit in Toronto before being sent overseas. She joined the Royal Canadian Army Medical Corps as a lieutenant nursing sister. I subsequently had many long exchanges with Bertha and over the years we became great pen pals. She sadly died in 2009 at the age of eighty-eight and I was sorry never to have met her. However, I did meet her granddaughters in 2005 while Bertha was still alive. Trista and Kayleigh came to stay with us in Warkworth, Northumberland, where Peter and I now live. They were lovely girls, and we had fun showing them around our local area. Tragically, Trista died in a road accident on 13 October 2006, a year after she had returned to Ontario from England.

Bertha gave me an insight into what it was like to work in the Canadian field hospital. In her letters, she talked about how they prepared to welcome the newborn babies. To make the cots, she said, they removed the wheels from the bottom of the "gurney" stretchers to make them more stable. They then borrowed dresser drawers from local people, which they put onto the gurney stretchers and made them into cosy little bassinets for the newborn babies. She told me that I started life in one of these drawers. Interestingly, when our daughter Bridgette was born, we made her a cot on legs out of the bottom drawer from an old chest. At that time, Peter was a university student, and we did not have enough money to buy a second cot. Stuart, only twenty months older than Bridgette, hadn't yet grown out of our main larger cot. It seemed a strange coincidence that our daughter and I both started our life in a drawer.

Bertha said she worked with a Dr Wallace Shute, and it was likely that he was the person who delivered me. He delivered most of the babies. This was the same doctor who signed my mother's confidential report when she gave me up for adoption. Dr Shute, from Ottawa, was known for making several significant contributions to medical science, particularly in the field of obstetrics. Bertha was still in touch with Wallace, and she told me that she mentioned my story to him. He was pleased to know that I had a happy life and was interested in the fact that I was searching for my birth mother. I began to feel that connections were beginning to form that might lead me to finding my mother.

In the hospital, Bertha told me, the little nursery was surrounded by rooms where wounded officers were being cared for and treated, some for horrific burns. One patient had been trapped inside a burning army tank. She described that the nurses were all too occupied to think about being scared during the war, even when German bombs fell. Despite working far away from the Germans' main target of London, Bertha recalled hearing the occasional buzz bombs that pounded the south of England in the latter stages of the war. These buzz bombs were winged German V-1 flying bombs, powered by jet engines, often called Doodlebugs. What was so frightening about them, was the piercing screaming noise that could be heard from the ground. The fear of these bombs stemmed from the fact that their motor could be heard quite clearly overhead. Before dropping to the ground, when the fuel ran out, the motor would stop, and people below knew that the bomb was then coming their way. In one of her letters, she recalled how "...some of the bad images stay with you forever. Seeing young men suffering, losing arms, legs and eyesight was the worst. These Canadians came to Europe young and healthy and went home maimed and emotionally scarred".

Peter and I returned to our friends' house after visiting Bramshott. I had a mixed set of emotions and felt withdrawn from the conversation. I was trying to picture myself, as a tiny baby, with my mother just after I was born. What an unhappy time it must have been for her. I hoped I had been a good baby and hadn't added to her grief. Perhaps if I had cried all the time, she would have been pleased to hand me on. I suppose she was passing through Bramshott in a daze, going through the motions of something that she had to get done and dusted before she could move on with her life. Behind the practical side of organising an adoption, she must have been devastated at having to give up her firstborn baby.

More than likely, my mother was only at Bramshott for a couple of weeks before she moved to Alderbrook. That might have been when our lives parted, and I was taken to the children's home in Knightsbridge. I found it hard to link the thought of how I am today, compared to that baby being given up for adoption. I regard myself as a well-balanced, rational person and I have never put myself into the category of "abandoned baby". Was this a result of my personality or did I happen to take a logical view of the whole thing because of the way I had been brought up by my adoptive parents?

Chapter 15

On 26 September 1945, as stated on my birth certificate, my mother had given her place of residence as Alderbrook Park, Surrey. Peter and I were still staying with Vivienne and Brian. Their house was close to Alderbrook. I wanted to see the place where my mother had convalesced after giving birth to me. What I found out was that Alderbrook Park had been built in Victorian times and was set within a 340-acre parkland. However, the substantial twenty-three-bedroom country mansion was demolished in 1956, making way for a more modest building.

Alderbrook Park, like many stately homes in England, was requisitioned by the Ministry of Defence (MOD) during the Second World War. The requisitioned country houses were mostly used as hospitals or recuperation homes. The Royal Canadian Army Medical Corps had acquired Alderbrook and turned it into a convalescence hospital, with fifty beds to accommodate female Canadian servicewomen.

I could not find a telephone number to ring Alderbrook Park, so I plucked up the courage and set off to make an unannounced visit. I went with Vivienne, her son Richard and my son James. We drove up a long drive into the estate through attractive parkland with open fields on either side of the driveway. The house was on the top of a hill but not particularly striking. It was certainly not the mansion that I was expecting. Of course, the stately home where my mother stayed was long gone. We parked the car in the circular forecourt near the front door. I knocked on the door leaving the others behind in the car. A delightful, elderly gentleman opened the door of this modest building.

He invited me into an ante-room near a spacious kitchen. I explained that my mother had been here during the war, and I was curious to see where she had lived. We chatted about the war. After fifteen minutes or so I left, but not before he had invited me and those in the car to look round the terrace gardens and the lawns that spread out towards the extensive landscaped parkland. This area was much the same as it would have been in my mother's time. He allowed me to take photographs but not of the house. It was a little disappointing that I hadn't been able to experience the same home where my mother had been for her recovery after my birth. Instead, I had visited what I regarded as an ordinary, newish building.

We drove back to Vivienne's, with me feeling it had been an exciting outing nevertheless. Again, it did not bring my search any further forward, but it was another glimpse into my mother's world.

Just after we arrived back at our friends' house, our daughter Bridgette phoned from our home in Wakefield, to say that someone from CBC (Canadian Broadcasting Company) was trying to contact me. She had given him our friends' phone number. Within minutes, he phoned. He wanted to come to Wakefield the next day to film a half-hour television programme highlighting my search for my birth mother. CBC had picked up the CTV programme, following its short news item on the "War Babies" in which I had appeared. Thinking the exposure might lead me to my mother, it did not take me long to agree. I thought this would be the break I was looking for. The programme might nudge some wartime memories into the minds of people who may have known about my mother's pregnancy. Or make my mother aware that I was looking for her.

I explained to the CBC reporter that I was staying with friends in Hampshire and that we had visited Alderbrook Park that day. He was buoyant with this news and asked if we could visit the Park again the next day and do some filming. I thought this was possible, so long as the owners agreed. I was assured that this was part of the programme manager's job to contact Alderbrook to smooth the way and get the necessary permissions.

After the filming, CBC said that he would be back in touch once they had looked at the film footage. He added that they would still want to come and film me in Wakefield to make sure they had my full story. I was not convinced that he would get back in touch and we parted with me thinking I was unlikely to hear from him again. My unease was because as it happened, he hadn't obtained permission from Alderbrook Park to film. He had tricked me into allowing myself to be recorded in the parkland. I was horrified when I learnt after the footage had been taken that no authorisation had been given.

A few weeks later, in early May 1992, a person called Nancy Durham phoned me to say that she worked for CBC. She wanted to come to Wakefield to interview me as part of the programme that CBC was putting together.

Nancy turned out to be someone to whom I could relate. I felt respect for her as a journalist. She completed the programme, and it went out on prime-time Canadian television on 8 May 1992. Nancy spent many years in the Balkans as a BBC journalist covering the complicated developments after the fraught breakup of former Yugoslavia.

As with the previous television interview, I had been careful not to name my birth mother or to give away any of her details. CBC would not allow my mother's full name to be used. The CBC lawyers were worried about libel for defamation of character. They only had my side of the story and my word that the adoption had taken place. Although I did produce documentation, which they could have followed up.

Nobody watching the programme could accurately identify my mother. Nonetheless, if my mother had watched the programme, there were sufficient clues for her to guess that the person featured was her daughter. I followed this line with all my adverts and newspaper articles that were written during my search. After all, I had no idea of her family circumstances. I did not want anybody to confront her following the appearance of an article that indicated she was the mother of a war baby in England. It was likely that this tactic was hampering my search, but I wanted there to be no shocks to her family. An English woman blurting out her mother's name on a television screen was something that I wished to avoid. It never occurred to me that she might be reluctant to come forward and make herself known to me. Assuming, of course, that she was still alive.

Nothing happened after the CBC programme, which left me uncertain as to what to do next. I did not think there was much profit in pursuing the Bournemouth angle, which was the reception area where my mother was first sent on arrival in England. It might have been a line of historical interest, which could have enabled another piece of the jigsaw to fit into the puzzle. On the other hand, it would not progress my search. The obvious thing I needed to do next was to chase up the Parent Finders lead in Canada, and that is what I did.

Part 4:

—

Concealment and Persistence

Chapter 16

I t was May 1992, two years after my serious search started and around fourteen years since I had sent for my original birth certificate. This is when I decided to ask for renewed help from Parent Finders in Edmonton, Alberta. Parent Finders' rationale was, "to deny adult adoptees their own birth records or knowledge of their heritage is to deny them a basic human right". I shared these values and understood how important it was for thousands of adoptees to be able to trace their parents. I had first joined Parent Finders in February 1991, but somehow, we lost contact with each other. I wrote to them again in February 1992 for advice. Unfortunately, at that time, they had been unable to help with my search. But following my recent enquiry, Anna Lees, who had also been adopted in Canada, told me she was going to be my search consultant. After she had found her own birth parents, she started to work as a volunteer for Parent Finders and wanted to help others find their families.

Anna provided me with various addresses of publications and magazines in Canada, so that I could place enquiring adverts. None of this proved to be helpful. It became clear that Anna Lees found my case a bit daunting and my regard for Parent Finders began to wane. I did not want to be too critical as they were running on a shoestring and relying on volunteers. After all, I was based in England as opposed to Canada, so why should Parent Finders help me? As was the pattern, my search was not advancing. I seemed to hit yet another blockage. I had great support from Peter, but no one else showed much interest in what I was trying to achieve. As previously, some people offered the view that I should just leave well alone.

It could be that over the last few years I had been "fiddling" around the edges of my search, enjoying the journey but not aiming for the destination. I was afraid of hurting people, or was I afraid of failure, or was I afraid that I might not like what I found? Despite all these thoughts, I had the drive to continue with my search regardless of all my doubts.

Unexpectedly, I got a letter from someone called Joan Barth, who later became my saviour, and we began to develop regular contact. Unbeknown to me, Anna Lees had passed my name onto Joan, who was a fellow Parent Finders volunteer. Joan was apologetic as my Parent Finders file had been shifted around from one volunteer to another. But Joan assured me that she had now taken up my case and would be my new search consultant. Looking back now, I'm so grateful for our pen friend relationship, and she would be another person whom I would love to meet.

Strange connections occur in life, and Joan was someone who offered help which became so crucial to my future. Her letters were warm and considerate. Joan had been adopted and had found her birth mother ten years previously. She gave me her age so I worked out that she would have been born in 1936. In her letter she introduced herself by telling me all about her family. Her son's wife had just given birth to twins.

Joan was fascinated to read my file which included the article from the Toronto Globe and Mail newspaper from November 1991.

She said she was pleased to see a picture of me as she liked to put a face to a name.

Joan gave me an address of the City Library in Winnipeg, Manitoba. This is where my mother had been discharged from the RCAF in 1946. She thought that would be a good starting point for information for my search. She told me to ask them to look in the Henderson Directory for any address for my mother. These are historical directories containing addresses of individuals and businesses in the Prairie Provinces of Canada. They date back to 1905 and are used for all types of research.

There was the possibility that my mother might have stayed in Winnipeg after she was discharged from the military. Joan wondered if my mother was now married, which of course might involve a name change from Hamilton. I thought that was likely, but not to my father. I did follow Joan's suggestion and wrote to the library in Winnipeg. Disappointingly, it proved to be a dead end. In many ways, my search was like looking for a needle in a haystack. Joan took on the search and looked at the Henderson Directory for Alberta, where she found a lengthy list of Hamiltons. She sent me the list but none of the names matched my mother's home address that was given on my birth certificate. It was quite a long shot to think that any current address, at the time of my birth, would be the same fifty years later.

Joan was particularly fascinated by the strange linkage between my birth mother's name, of Elizabeth Jane Hamilton, and my own name at birth. My birth name was Donna Mary Hamilton, my adopted mother's family name was Hamilton, and my adoptee name was Catherine Elizabeth Hamilton Pattinson. She asked me if I was sure that there was no family Hamilton connection that I hadn't been told about. It did seem to be such an unusual coincidence. Just to double check, I wrote to my adoptive mother's cousin, Chiquita

Cullip, in Australia, the only family link to my mother who was still alive. It turned out to be just a fascinating twist of fate with no link between the two families. I do feel pleased and comforted by the fact that the Hamilton name has been a cornerstone in my life.

In another letter, Joan told me that she had done some further research in the Edmonton library. In 1943, an Elizabeth Hamilton lived at the address which was listed on my birth certificate. Four years later, there was a record of Elizabeth Hamilton living at a different place in Edmonton. There was a connection as these addresses were owned by a Frank Hamilton. It was possible that this Elizabeth Hamilton could be my mother, and Frank could be her father. It could equally have been her brother or uncle, but it seemed more likely that Frank was her father. All this took me a step forward and other questions came into my mind about whether my existence was known within the family.

This latest development in my search brought about a strange nervousness. I found myself thinking more deeply about the disturbing position in which my mother would have found herself when it became obvious that she was pregnant. My RCAF father whom she named in the Westminster documents, had returned to his home in Canada at the end of the war. I had a feeling that he had gone home to continue his life, without my mother.

I was glad that I had learnt that I was adopted when I was young. I imagine it would be a much more disturbing discovery if I had found out, say, on my wedding day or on the birth of my first child, or even worse after my adoptive parents had both died. Living into adulthood and then learning that you were adopted I thought might be much more difficult to confront. That would seem to seriously interfere with the notion of who you thought you were. As a teenager, at times, I found it exciting to imagine who my mother might be.

Joan asked me to write to a Mr John Oldring, who was the Minister of Family and Social Services in Alberta. Parent Finders were desperately trying to change the law on adoption records that were covered by the Canadian Privacy Act. They needed all the support they could get. They particularly appreciated the help from those who were actively searching for their birth parents.

The letter I received back from Mr Oldring appeared to follow the political line at the time, of procrastination and polite obstruction. The letter said that they were watching the changes that were being introduced in other jurisdictions, both in Canada and abroad. They were considering what changes might seem appropriate for Alberta. They were dealing with the challenges of striking a balance between those who wished to preserve their anonymity against those who wanted complete unrestricted access to sealed records. The letter was courteous, saying that my concerns would be considered in their review. Once again, it felt as if the innocent child had no voice in any legal proceedings that affected them deeply. It was understandable that a mother needed privacy and protection. However, this should be weighed against the innocent child having an equal right to establish their identity. I'm convinced that honesty and openness should be the only way forward. Although, on occasions, I appreciate that the child might need protection from their natural parents. This is a completely different scenario to mine and it should be treated with care. The circumstances of the child should be taken into consideration above everything else. The safety of the welfare of the child being paramount. I was presuming that I was not born out of rape or abuse. How does anyone cope with that information?

My next letter from Joan turned out to be crucial in my search. For the first time in years, I was looking at key evidence that revealed details of my mother's family. This lead was more exciting than I could have imagined. It was hard to take in how suddenly, after so much time, Joan was pointing me in the direction of my mother's whereabouts. It erupted out of nowhere and suddenly it seemed such an easy piece of discovery. Despite the Canadian privacy laws, here was Joan, opening the door to where my mother might be.

Chapter 17

Feelings of excitement, apprehension and relief all burst off the page of Joan's letter. As I repeatedly read the letter it dawned on me that I was now closer than ever before to finding my birth mother. For me, as great as my adoptive parents were, the anxiety and wondering who really brought me into the world is something that has constantly gnawed away at the back of my mind. Making that maternal connection, which is not always possible for many people, is such a basic urge that can be hard to describe for those not in that position.

The day before Joan's letter arrived, I was particularly despondent. I still had hardly any more information than when I'd started my search. My, presumed, in-depth research had been running for four years. I had tried to follow every avenue that had been suggested to me. But I had come up against so many brick walls. I had reached a stage where I was thinking that I would never find my birth mother. Joan's letter instantly swept away all my frustrations and disappointments. She had followed quite a straightforward piece of research. I can now only say how easy it was with the benefit of hindsight. It made all my earlier efforts part of a convoluted journey going to nowhere. The key to unlocking the door was having someone in Canada able to research in the location where my birth family lived.

It was Saturday 26 September 1992 when I read Joan's letter outlining the information she had found in the Edmonton library. It came from a 1972 newspaper article in the Edmonton Journal. It was an obituary for a Frank Hamilton, aged eighty. It said that his wife Elizabeth Hamilton had been buried in the previous year. Listed, were all their children and the towns where they were living. There were eight children, two boys and the rest girls. None of the girls had the Hamilton surname, which indicated that they were all married. I scanned the list that Joan had so carefully written out in her letter, but there was no Elizabeth. The only Elizabeth Hamilton was Frank's wife, and her age did not fit the profile of my mother. But then there was a Bessie O'Brien listed as living in Vancouver. Bessie was short for Elizabeth, and Hamilton would have been her maiden name. This explained why I hadn't got far with my search. Although I guessed she might have married, I had no way of knowing what her married name would be. I was trying to locate an Elizabeth Jane Hamilton in Edmonton when I should have been searching for Bessie O'Brien in Vancouver.

Listed amongst my uncles and aunts were two brothers and a sister who lived in Edmonton. Another sister from Port Hueneme in California, and a sister in Grand Prairie. There were two further sisters in Vancouver, making a total of eight siblings. I was excited about being a member of a large family, which was something I had always wanted. When I married, I thought I would like six children. However, I changed my views after three pregnancies – they all made me horribly sick. I felt sympathy for any woman giving birth to many babies, year after year.

Despite all the latest information, I was feeling nervous about finding my mother. There was the sensitive issue of not wanting to barge into an established family. How do you break the news of an abandoned baby in England? To try and narrow the search,

Peter and I looked through the list of my mother's siblings for any unusual surnames, so that we would not come across hundreds in a telephone directory. We decided it would be helpful to pick a sibling from a small town. We hoped this would make the tracing easier. I liked this idea and besides, suddenly, I was happy to have an excuse not to confront my birth mother just yet. Was I still enjoying the journey and frightened to arrive at the destination?

Joan had given me a telephone number thinking this might be my aunt, in Edmonton. Having just taken delivery of Joan's letter, I was too nervous to telephone the number. Peter said he would ring. His disguise, to keep the trail away from me, was to say he was from the British Legion and was trying to contact Canadians posted to England during the Second World War. It was to offer an invitation to a commemorative event in London. It soon became obvious that this woman had no connection with my mother. The next day I did nothing. From the promising developments of the previous day, I was beginning to think that I might be starting on the merry-go-round again and get nowhere.

The following evening Peter persuaded me to have another go at picking a name from the list of my uncles and aunts. At this point, I was still not mentally ready to make actual contact with my mother in Vancouver. I was torn emotionally as I did not want the trail to go cold. Peter thought we should try and track down my aunt in Port Hueneme in California. Peter also had the idea of telephoning his uncle, who lived in Vancouver, to see how many O'Briens were listed in the city. His uncle did not answer the call, so no joy there. However, his uncle was blind, so it would be difficult for him to find names without help anyway. My aunt's surname in California, was Broadchurch. We thought surely there could not be many families with that name in the Californian town. What I later found out that Port Hueneme was a large US naval base with more than 19,000 personnel. On contacting international directory enquiries, they told Peter there was no such name listed. So that was the end of that promising lead. If we had done a bit more research into the area, we would have worked out that those living on a naval base were unlikely to have their personal details listed in a local directory.

Moving down the sibling list, our next port of call was a place called Grand Prairie in British Columbia. We thought this was likely to be a small quiet town, with not too many names in the directory. The time difference in British Columbia is eight hours behind Britain, therefore a perfect time for Peter to call would be in the evening UK time. The surname we were looking for was Jones. Directory enquiries said that there were two people called Jones listed in the town. We noted down the two numbers and Peter made the call.

As Peter tried the first of the two Joneses, I sat at our kitchen table in trepidation. I could not face listening to what was being said. I felt like a mischievous child, taking part in something that was none of my business. I was intruding into someone else's life. With the first call, luck had it that contact had been made with the right Jones. My mother's brother-in-law, Will Jones, answered the telephone. His wife, my aunt, had died a year or so before. Peter gave the same story about the British Legion that he had used before. Without the need for too much subterfuge, Will gave Peter my mother's telephone number, listed as Bessie O'Brien. Will confirmed that she had formerly been called Elizabeth Jane Hamilton, and she was over in Britain during the War. The conversation was not long, and the call soon ended.

Peter walked into the kitchen with a piece of paper in his hand. He quietly put the paper on the table in front of me, giving me my mother's name and telephone number. And that was it, I had found her. She was still alive. I felt stunned. We sat for just a few moments in silence. Lots of jumbled thoughts rushed around inside my head. Here I was at 47 years of age, with the details sitting on the table, that would allow me, for the first time, to have a conversation with my birth mother. I had a surge of exhilaration, then I was quickly overwhelmed by trepidation and panic, not knowing how to react to this immensely important telephone number. I sat too petrified to do anything.

Peter broke the silence and suggested that I ring my birth mother. Fear and sudden uncontrollable nervousness had taken a firm hold of me. I was not tearful, I just felt numb. I told Peter I could not ring my mother. It was too sudden. I was not ready. I needed time to digest the information and think about what to do next. I feared this piece of paper that Peter had put in front of me. So little detail really with nothing more than a telephone number, but this was huge to me after nearly fifty years of uncertainty. There was a lot to take in, but here I was, at last, talking about the woman who had given birth to me, knowing she was just at the end of a telephone line. I could not think straight, other than I should leave the moment of discovery to sink in and to see if it was still real the next morning.

When I walk along the street, I look at young men, who would be around the same age as Stuart. I wonder how he would have developed and how he would have lived his life. Would my mother also do the same about me? I glance at women who would be the same age as my birth mother, and think what she must be like now, as an older woman. I rehearse in my mind what it would feel like if I ever met her. I'm a mature woman with a family, and I wonder what we might have in common apart from my birth. It struck me that she may still carry the guilt of giving her baby away. Thoughts came into my head as to how she would have moved on in her life and, perhaps, not thinking about me at all. In which case, she would not welcome my reappearance in her world.

Once again, I had the nagging worry about whether I was doing the right thing. It was a genuine question as to whether I should intrude into my birth mother's life. On the other hand, there was the question of whether I should impose this upheaval onto Bridgette and James. The thought crossed my mind that it might uncover something distasteful or disturbing. I considered what my friends might think and if they would even be interested. When I went to bed that night I had a disturbed sleep. I took the piece of paper to bed with me and put it under my pillow as I was fearful of losing the precious telephone number.

Peter's cousin Michael and his family had been living in Vancouver for several years. We decided that the next step was for Peter to give Michael a ring to see if he could put an address to the telephone number that Peter had been given by my newfound uncle. Michael said he would do a bit of detective work to try and pin her location down. About ten minutes later, he telephoned back to say he had found her under E J O'Brien. E J signifying Elizabeth Jane. It was only her name attached to the apartment, so she was either divorced or her husband had died.

The next part of the plan was for Michael, and his wife Daphne, to visit the address on the pretext that they had got lost while trying to deliver some flowers. With a bunch of flowers in Daphne's hand, Michael knocked on my mother's apartment door. A friendly chatty woman spoke to them at length. Michael can be charming and was good at telling a tale. This achieved four things. It confirmed beyond doubt, that it was my mother. It proved that she was alive and of sound mind. And there was every sign that she lived alone. If I sent her a letter, the chances were that she would not be opening it at the breakfast table in front of anyone else. She would have time to take in the contents quietly on her own. It had always been important to avoid the presence of a husband, or someone close to her, being there when a letter was opened announcing the existence of her long-lost daughter in England. The problem that it could create was something I wanted to avoid.

What had been a puzzle for so long, was now unravelling with the latest telephone call from Michael. He told me of the existence of a small, trim, lively lady with a smile enriched by her dimples. I felt a combination of emotions that included mental exhaustion, shock and elation. That I had found my mother after years of searching was an incredible experience. I had got this treasured information, and I wanted to sit back and savour it. I needed to keep it safe in case somebody might take it away from me or I might lose it, or it would suddenly become unreal. It was a lot for me to handle. There was still an odd feeling of rejection but balanced against an overwhelming emotion of discovery. I could telephone right there and then but I wanted nothing to do with the telephone for fear of not knowing what to say. Making that telephone call, if I ever plucked up courage to do it, might make me hear things I did not like. The person on the other end of the telephone could appear as a stranger, a friend or just simply my mother. I had surmounted what I thought was the main hurdle in my quest, only to realise that a major part of the journey was still in front of me. There were clearly difficulties ahead. In my search I had always felt in control. Now I was decidedly out of my comfort zone, and I was uneasy about contacting my birth mother.

Chapter 18

I did nothing for a few days. My mind was in turmoil, and I was not prepared for feeling so emotional. I was high up on a mountain, where the oxygen was sparse. I floundered around for guidance. I listened to advice from friends. I read articles about the experience of those who had been adopted and found their birth parents. I thought I would feel more calm and able to cope with the situation. It surprised me that I was struggling to deal with the conflicting voices reverberating in my head. Should I be doing this? What might the consequences be?

After a few days of reflection, I managed to take back control of my senses. I decided to write a letter, telling my birth mother that I was alive and well and that this was her daughter trying to make contact after forty-seven years. The letter was dated Wednesday 30 September 1992, just four days after receiving Joan's letter. It seemed more like ten weeks rather than a few days. In with the letter, I enclosed the video of the programme that CBC had made earlier in the year. I decided that it might help her to know a little about my life. I sent the package by Swift Air and by registered post from our village Post Office. Handing the letter over the post office counter was like letting go of something so precious. The envelope was being swept into unknown territory, now out of my control. I then wrote to Joan, thanking her for all her diligent investigations. Without Joan I would still have been stumbling around getting more frustrated.

When writing the letter to my mother, I thought the only way, after all these years, was to be open and honest. I had been deceitful enough with the newspaper articles, the television programmes, the tale that Peter and I had concocted to her brother-in-law and finally, the visit from Daphne and Michael to her apartment.

Before penning the letter, I spent the day considering all the different approaches and the recommendations given by various organisations for the first contact with a birth parent. I ended up writing what I instinctively felt was right for me and hoped that my mother would feel the same way. I chose my words carefully, pondering long and hard over the contents of the letter.

After sending the letter, any further development was now out of my hands. I had to sit and wait and hope that my mother would respond soon. I felt mentally drained and could not allow myself to feel excited until I received a positive response from my birth mother. I missed my adoptive parents who had both died ten years previously. The sneaky feeling of being disloyal to them kept creeping into my head. I wished my adoptive mother were alive so that I could talk to her. I knew that might have been unkind, as I would have used her as an emotional prop to lean on. It would not have been fair to her after everything she had done for me during my life. She had loved me all my life and we were close in our own way. There had never been many cuddles or outward signs of sentiment. Rather, it was more of a practical, honest, solid relationship.

While waiting for a reply to my letter, I was in limbo. There was a strange feeling that part of me was being reborn, getting a chance to start again. At last, I had made contact with my birth mother.

A month went by, and I heard nothing. I fully appreciated that my mother might not respond. The case studies that I read suggested that many birth mothers were reluctant to acknowledge their children. But I was sure my mother must share some of my feelings. Not a sentimental rosy view on a mother and daughter relationship, but more an instinctive curiosity of wanting to know about her daughter. Even if in 1945 she did not have much time to bond with me, I was still her child. The silence seemed especially sad, given that she would be seventy and getting to the evening of her life. Maybe she could not get this skeleton out of her cupboard, given the passage of nearly half a century. Was the shame of my birth so deep rooted? It seemed to me that she should not be criticised over a mistake that she had made so many years ago. The silence was perplexing.

I was in the position where I could pick up the telephone and speak to her, but I found I could not do that. The feeling of rejection was ever present. In one sense I felt alone, and I needed her to pick up the telephone or for her to write to tell me she was delighted to find her daughter. I could not push my way into her life and demand recognition. That would deny me ever knowing whether she genuinely wanted to grasp that piece of her life that she believed she had left buried with such anguish all those years ago.

I was close to the end of the long journey that I began with such enthusiasm after I got my original birth certificate in 1978. Fourteen years had passed. I was now facing the fact that my mother wanted nothing to do with me. I flinched every time the telephone rang, thinking it might be her. I pretended to act casually when the postman dropped the mail through the letterbox, yet underneath, I was simmering with excitement. But now, the prevailing feeling was emptiness. I invented a hundred stories as to why she hadn't written back to say how happy she was to have found me. The intoxicating joy and bewilderment of discovery had turned to excited expectation, and then to mystery as to why I was not getting a response. My exciting journey began to lose its lustre and hope turned to disappointment.

I was preparing to face the harsh reality that my mother was not rushing to write to me, let alone speak to me or even, one day, meet me. I had been floating on a balloon, and now the air was leaking out and I was plummeting to earth. All the anticipation was fizzing away. Setting off on what I thought was a fairy tale journey was a bit childish. As reality dawned, I discovered that this was no childhood story. I still managed to cling to the belief that somehow, in some way, my mother would make contact.

But by November 1992, two months after I had sent my letter to my birth mother, I had resigned myself to not hearing from her. Trying to force the issue, if she did not want to make contact, was never going to work. The rejection was profound, and I had to deal with it. However, Peter had other ideas. Over the last few weeks, he was pushing me to let him telephone my mother to find out the situation. Daphne and Michael wanted to visit her again to see if she really wanted nothing to do with me. I felt I could not allow Peter to telephone or Daphne and Michael to visit. It had to be on mine and my mother's terms. I did not want anyone else taking the lead on something that emotionally belonged to a mother and her daughter. I was not going to be jostled into action. The situation had to run its course for better or worse. I was prepared to accept the outcome. If I could deal with the worst thing in my life – Stuart dying – then I could deal with this.

Peter eventually wore me down and I agreed that he should telephone my mother. So, on 22 November 1992 he made the call. The main house telephone was in the hall sitting on a table, made from an old treadle sewing machine, next to the front door and near the stairs. There was an extension to the phone in the kitchen. This is where Peter sat to make the call while I went upstairs. I did not want to hear the conversation, so I lay on our bed, apprehensive as to what the outcome of the call would be. My mother answered the phone.

After the conversation ended, Peter called me downstairs. He thought the exchange with my mother had gone exceptionally well. He told me that she had received my letter but soon after it arrived, she went away on a month's cruise to Japan. After that she meant to reply but did not have the opportunity to do so. I listened intently as Peter relayed the conversation. To me this was a significant point in my journey, but it did not seem so important for my mother. Immediate contact was not high on her agenda. She went on to say she had been married and was now divorced and that she had two daughters who lived on Vancouver Island. They were, as expected, younger than me. She described her family and said she was closest to her elder sister, Sal, who also lived in Vancouver. Sal knew all about me. She said she was always known as Bessie, as her mother was called Elizabeth. She was born in Ireland in 1922. At the age of six, the family had emigrated to Edmonton in Canada. She joined the RCAF in 1943 and was posted to Britain in 1944. After returning to Canada, she settled in Vancouver in September 1946. This was where she met and married the father of her other two girls. They had been divorced for twenty years. At the time of my birth, she said she told nobody except her four closest friends who were with her in London. These friends were Marg, Mary, Glady and Jessie. She was particularly close to Marg and Mary.

My mother described my birth as "not particularly unhappy". Her friends helped her through her pregnancy and the after-effects of my birth. She breastfed me for the first two weeks of my life. After these first two weeks, she then put me in the home in Knightsbridge where she waited for me to be adopted. She described how she had to pay for this home and knew that I had been adopted when the payments ceased.

She recalled how she became aware that I was looking for her, when one of her brothers, Doug, visited her from Edmonton and gave her the Edmonton Journal cutting. This, of course, was written by me asking for an Elizabeth Jane Hamilton to make contact. The advertisement was purposely obscure and hadn't mentioned England and simply gave a Box contact number with my name Catherine Atkinson. She had sensed that this was her lost daughter from England who had placed the advert. My mother said she was able to deflect attention away from Doug's questioning about who this person could be. She offered the view that someone must be trying to contact their mother, my grandmother, who was also called Elizabeth Hamilton. My advert had used the full name of Elizabeth Jane, but they put that down to the fact that the advert writer was confused. My grandmother had died by the time my advert reached Edmonton, and so no more attention was paid to the matter. Keeping it to herself, my mother said she realised at that point that I was on the search. Peter got the impression that Bessie was not in a rush to respond to my letter. She had covered up her secret for so long that it had become instinctive for her to maintain her concealment.

Peter told me she was fit and well and sounded positive and sensible. He said she had a practical tone in her voice and seemed calm during the conversation, although a little taken aback at first. She was content to answer all the questions on the telephone and was in no rush to put the receiver down. She promised to send a picture of herself and would write in a few days. She repeated that she was not too surprised about being found, because she had realised that I was on her trail and Peter's call was not a bolt out of the blue. Funnily enough, the Edmonton Journal advert had, quite co-incidentally, been published on 11 September, which is my birthday, and the date had resonated with her.

My mother recounted she had been back to Britain, a few times, to visit her cousins in Northern Ireland. On one of these trips, she had a vague plan in her mind to travel to London from Northern Ireland to look up the adoption home in Knightsbridge, but she never went through with it. She told Peter it would be too much to speak to me on the telephone, preferring to ease herself into the relationship with a letter first. I was secretly pleased about that, because like her, I was not ready to talk. Peter thought my mother sounded as though she wanted to move the relationship on a bit further but only slowly. I got Peter to tell me, repeatedly, every minute detail of the conversation. I needed to draw from him every nuance of the exchange, missing absolutely nothing from the dialogue. The joyful reunion that I had invented, would have to be put on hold or never happen.

As a first step, a written reply from my mother seemed to be the best form of contact between us. I suddenly felt happy that my mother had said, positively, that she would write to me. This made me want to smile all the time, even in my sleep. It was such a relief not to have that sense of rejection hanging around anymore. Like many adoptees, whether it's justified or not, I felt that being put up for adoption was an act of rejection. I realised this is over-simplifying things. Mothers giving children up for adoption have a range of complicated reasons for doing so. It did not mean there was an outright rejection of their child nor that they did not overwhelmingly love their baby. Once having made some contact with my mother, it would be hard to take if she actively said she wanted nothing to do with me. But the telephone call had gone well, and I was over another hurdle. I now had an element of inner calm from knowing that she did not mind the contact, at least with Peter.

Chapter 19

The telephone call to my mother left me with a longing to get the whole matter of my adoption out in the open. It was if I had been tiptoeing around the issue all my life. Now, I knew I had two half-sisters, and I wanted to meet them. I was concerned, however, that my mother would not get round to telling them. The knowledge of those sisters was extremely important to me. I was starting to have a firm feeling of 'belonging', which I wanted openly declared. My birth mother appeared level-headed; I yearned for her to progress down a similar path to mine, which was not wanting the secret dominating our lives anymore.

I became excited and thrilled at the idea of receiving a letter and hopefully a photograph of my birth mother. I needed to share the news that Peter had spoken to her. Again, the one person I wanted to speak to was my adoptive mother. I was convinced she would have been as excited as I was. I hoped she would not have felt, in any way, that she was not my mother anymore. She was the only mother I had known and loved, and it was always going to still be that way.

During the conversation Peter had with my birth mother, she said she was going to write and enclose a photograph. But a month later, nothing had happened. It was now into December 1992, and there was no sign of my mother making any contact. My first letter, along with the video, had been sent on 30 September and Peter's telephone call had been on 22 November.

I received a Christmas letter from a friend in Australia called Wendy, who had also been adopted as a baby. Earlier that year, Wendy was tracked down by her half-sister, who she did not know existed. The sister told Wendy she had been adopted and had traced their shared birth mother. She wanted to meet Wendy and for them both to see their mother. Wendy was different from me; she had no interest in ever finding her birth mother. It turned out that her mother wanted her past to be kept a secret. Her mother had put a clause in her file saying she did not want to be found. This made Wendy uncertain about meeting her half-sister and birth mother. She eventually agreed for her sister to organise a get-together. The meeting was arranged quickly, too quickly for Wendy's comfort, and just by coincidence, it happened to fall on Wendy's forty-first birthday. They met and Wendy described it "as a mix of incredible emotions", not all of them particularly welcome. After the reunion, they only met one more time and had no interest in each other's lives.

Wendy's letter was hard to read because, once again, she made me question whether I was doing the right thing by my birth mother. Wendy's situation had many parallels to mine, but she was blatantly coming at her adoption from a far more unsettled position. Her approach was more about avoiding any confrontation and not wanting to disturb the past. Whereas I was interested in wanting to build a consenting bridge and mend something that carried with it an amount of pain. And to stop the unhappiness that three mothers had suffered.

All along, Peter and I stayed in touch with Michael, Peter's cousin in Vancouver. Michael's wife Daphne persuaded me it might be helpful if she went round to my mother's apartment to speak to her, woman to woman, face to face as it were. With the likelihood fading of receiving any letter, I agreed, and Daphne duly went round to my mother's apartment on the 11 December. She was hoping to get an understanding of how my mother was thinking after the contact from her first born. I was at work at Huddersfield University, where I was a Principal Lecturer in Textile Design, when Daphne's fax came through saying the meeting had been successful. She mentioned that the video I had sent to my mother was not in a suitable format for her to be able to view on a Canadian player. Daphne took the video. She told her that Michael was in the film industry and would be able to "dub" the tape into the correct format for my mother to play it on her television.

Daphne's short fax reassured me that she had a positive session with my mother, but I needed to know more. After a period of self-doubt, I telephoned Daphne in the hope that she might be able to put my mind at rest that my mother would eventually make contact. Daphne described my mother as small and slim and being a lively, active woman who often went sailing with a man friend. My mother had described that ninety percent of her time was taken up working for the forces Legion Club in Vancouver, where she was the first lady President. Not long ago, she had retired from her work in a solicitor's office in Vancouver. She had lived in Vancouver since 1946. She was now seventy.

My mother confided in Daphne that she had gone to England to join the war just to please her father. She was close to her father who had been a military man. He was disappointed that his two sons were too young to join up, so she volunteered to go instead. It's not easy to get your head around the notion of going to war just to please your father. If times had been different and if she hadn't been overseas, she said that her pregnancy would have resulted in her keeping me. But, with her military circumstances in England, she felt it was just not possible for her to return home with a baby, especially when her father had held her up as a hero. Daphne felt sure I would hear from her soon, although it might take a little time for her to adjust to the idea and I had to be patient. I was good at being patient as I had been doing it for years. Daphne said that to be realistic, I should not expect to hear anything before the end of January 1993.

My mother had just returned from the funeral of her brother-in-law in California, and she would then spend Christmas with her two daughters on Vancouver Island. Daphne explained that her daughters still did not know of my existence and this, for my mother, was a major sticking point. I had wondered earlier what would happen if she never told them. Such reluctance to tell them might put her off contacting me. Their feelings were at the top of her priority list. I was well buried, and it was easier for her to leave it that way. For almost fifty years, she had harboured the secret of my birth from those who were important to her. She could continue to delude herself by keeping me in the shadows. I suppose Peter and Daphne were the first people to confront her with my existence since I was a baby. So far, she had kept me at arm's length. She was protecting herself by not owning up to the fact that I had any place in her life. In a roundabout way, this threw all the guilt back onto me. I was far from an equal partner in this epic story.

After Daphne's contact with my mother, I wrote a short letter to my mother enclosing a Christmas card and a present. The present was a Liberty's of London photo frame and a Liberty scarf. I thought she might appreciate something from the famous London department store. It might bring back memories of her time in London during the war. My hope was that these memories were happy ones. Time moved on to early 1993 and I waited until the end of January, as Daphne had suggested, before expecting any communication from my mother. After all, some people are poor at letter writing and just never quite get round to it. The end of January came and went with nothing.

By this stage, I was getting anxious over the whole affair. I was guilt-ridden on account of the family having to put up with me being so preoccupied with my search. I tried hard not to let it dominate our lives. Some of my friends, and perhaps Bridgette and James, had either become bored or immune to my pursuit. I tried hard to understand how my mother might be feeling. I believed that it was only a matter of time before she would come round to accepting me. On the other hand, back came the old thoughts about whether I was going to be in the two per cent category of those whose mothers wanted nothing to do with them.

On Sunday 7 February 1993 I decided to write again; this time it was a long letter giving her more of my family background and describing how I felt about her. It was handwritten and nine pages long. I started at the beginning of my search when I had obtained my original Birth Certificate. I tried to explain to her how I felt about my adoption. I told her that I had grown up accepting that I must bear the guilt of being an "illegitimate child" in silence. I described my adoptive parents and my adoptive brother. I told her about Stuart and the effect it had on our family. I discussed in the letter that I understood her need to have me adopted and I placed no blame on her. I might have done the same if I had been in her shoes. I thanked her for not having an abortion. I said I was happy and well balanced and adored my husband and my children. Overall, I was content to have been bought up in Britain and my life had been good.

My intention, in the letter, was not to harass her but to tell her how it was with me. I then went on to tell her that I realised my letter was packed with emotion and that my arrival on her scene will have come as a shock. I said it may seem as if my contact with her had happened suddenly, but the fact was, for me, it had been fifteen years of searching and a lifetime of wondering.

In my letter I did not want to convey the impression that I was underestimating how she might feel. I recognised the pain she would have suffered in giving me away at birth. I wanted her to know that I thought I understood how she must be feeling, having virtually buried me all those years ago. She would have had to do that to mentally survive. I acknowledged how difficult it must be to tell her two daughters of my existence. I wondered how I could reappear as her daughter if she could not tell her family. I talked more about Stuart dying and how she could never meet her eldest grandchild and how sad I felt about that. I went on to say that not knowing where I came from, for me, was difficult to understand.

However, I thought she should go with her instincts and react as she felt best for her and her family. I added I was proud of the way that she had coped with my adoption at the end of the war and being in a foreign country. In the letter I finished by chatting about the children and Peter. I told her that I might telephone in a few weeks when she would have had time to absorb my letter. I said to her that I would like to come to Vancouver to meet her.

After I sent the letter, I sensed that I might still receive no response. By now it was March 1993, and I could wait no longer. I would have to take decisive action to move the situation forward and I could not face the possibility that my search might end here.

Chapter 20

In the Spring of 1993, I began to lose hope. Any direct contact between me and my birth mother was not happening. It was September 1992 when I had first written to her and now, six months later, I was in touching distance of my goal and yet so far away. It was like the repeat of a bad dream.

Now I was at another low point. I had sent letters and photographs, a Christmas card and a present, and yet I had received nothing back. Over the months I rationalised to myself why my mother hadn't made contact. In a way, I was defending her position and concealing my own vulnerability. I became practised at keeping my feelings of being upset and wanting to cry under control. Mostly I managed to do this, as I was working full-time, and the family needed a happy Mum and wife. Nevertheless, the doubts of self-worth were hard to shift. After all I was intruding into my birth mother's life. She hadn't asked for it and did not welcome my interference into what I perceived to be her cosy world. I did not feel angry at her lack of correspondence or telephone calls, just sadness.

The unreasonably long wait to hear from my mother not only led me to dwell on the death of Stuart, but the self-reproach I felt about betraying my adoptive mother. On top of it all, I had the sense of being rebuffed by my birth mother who just would not respond. I recognise that I have a strong practical side to my personality, and I do have an inbuilt coping ability. This was responsible for me disguising a lot of my feelings. I'm quite comfortable talking about emotional issues, but I'm well practised at hiding any deep intense reactions and placing them quietly in a box. I get exasperated with myself if I think I'm being selfish, self-indulgent, or overdramatic. That is when I put 'stuff' in the box, and it's difficult to bring it back out again and to confront the issues that are just under the surface. The only person that could help me through this kind of despondent phase was myself. Tears were never an answer.

Months earlier, at the end of December 1992, I had written to Joan Barth from Parent Finders to keep her up to date as to the progress on making contact with my birth mother. She replied at once and was glad to have received my letter. She was pleased that Daphne, Peter's cousin's wife, had made personal contact with my mother, and that Peter had had a couple of positive conversations with her over the telephone. Joan thought it was right that I had written a few times even though there was no reply. 'Give it time' was the message I was getting from everyone.

More tortuous weeks passed by. I waited to see if my mother would respond to my letters. A sort of "fait accompli" had set into my thoughts, with the real possibility that I might never make personal contact with her. But by the end of March 1993, I had to bring matters to a head. Despite being nervous, I plucked up courage and telephoned her.

My mother answered the telephone and was charming and friendly. I instantly related to her in a relaxed and comfortable way. She was warm and seemed genuinely pleased to hear from me and sounded sincere. We spoke for forty minutes. We got on well. She was easy to talk to and she asked lots of questions about the children. She was extremely sympathetic when I mentioned Stuart. We talked about the war and her children and her marriage. She was sorry she hadn't written but she had started lots of letters and then never sent them. If I'm honest, I'm not sure I totally believed that bit. What I did believe was, that she genuinely had wanted to write to me. She told me she had got some photographs together with the intention of, sometime in the future, putting them in the post. She confirmed she was not good at letter writing and preferred to chat on the telephone. However, she promised me she would now send the photos.

My mother told me she was active and walked a lot. She had given up work two years earlier at the age of sixty-nine. Also, she said she was about to go on holiday with five other "girls" to Reno, gambling. Now, that did take me by surprise. We then talked about her two other daughters. She confessed that she thought she might never be able to tell them of my existence. She concluded they might be angry. She was still so ashamed about what had happened to her in London during the war. She wanted me to remain as her dark secret, although she sounded genuinely moved and happy that I had made contact.

I asked her about coming to Vancouver to meet her, even if it was just for a cup of coffee. She knew about Daphne and Michael and that I had somewhere to stay. She agreed this might be a good idea. After being so anxious about the call, I felt such relief as I put the telephone down. I was pleased I had done it and was now shaking after being so keyed up. I was relieved that she did not deny me being her daughter. She sounded pleasant, and the call could not have gone better. I remember thinking how odd it was that my own mother had a strange accent.

I was glad I had plucked up courage to speak on the telephone and this was the way forward. My instincts had been right that she did not really "do" letters. I should have spotted that earlier. When I was speaking to her, it was as if I had known her for a long time. I was conscious of how difficult it must have been for her to accept me as her adult child. I was not the baby she had left behind all those years ago. She would picture me as an infant, not as I was now, a grown woman. There was nothing about me now that could possibly resemble the little bundle at birth. She might imagine me as a threat to her lifestyle. Presumably, she never thought about the problem of confronting me later in life when she gave me up for adoption in a foreign country. I just hoped that the process of accepting me was not going to be too painful for her. I envisaged she must be feeling frightened about having to tell her family. Maybe she was overwhelmed by this fear and frozen to the point that she became powerless to respond when my first letter arrived. I wondered whether my mother would ever be able to peel away the layers of her guilt. I imagined she might have the same fears of rejection as I had, she thinking of the possibility of being boycotted by her family and me being shunned by her. It was a tricky situation for both of us to face.

I was convinced that although my mother had 'lost' me after my birth, time might bring about her wanting to meet me. To have your child adopted and then refuse to meet that child as an adult, seemed to me, tantamount to a double loss.

Over the years, I had kept in touch with Nancy Durham, the journalist from the Canadian Broadcasting Corporation who had interviewed me for the Canadian television documentary, which had gone out across Canada in May 1992. Nancy's thoughts, on my mother not writing to me, were like my own in that she found it incredibly difficult to understand how somebody would not want to contact their long-lost daughter. Like me, she felt that I was right to keep going and not to give up. In her letter, she told me her theory that, with my mother, it was like a man who does not have the nerve to ask his girlfriend to marry him, whilst inside that is what he really wants. That meant that the girlfriend had to do all the work in pushing for a wedding. This rang a bell with me, in that Peter had needed a tiny bit more than just a nudge to get us to the altar.

I kept my contact with Joan Barth, as she stayed interested in my developments in relation to my mother. I kept her up to date in that, so far, no letter had yet arrived from Vancouver. Because of the lack of any progress, I made my second telephone call to Canada in May 1993. Another matter was beginning to worry me. I was now getting a bit stuck in my own mind about how I had ended up with two mothers. Now it was my turn to have a mental block because I hadn't really worked out how to cope with this. Being comfortable with the right name may sound trivial, but when you have spent your life calling your adopted mother, Mummy, what do you then call your birth mother when she appears on the scene. Until this point, I hadn't really had to face this dilemma. What would feel right, Mother, Mum, Mummy or Mom? I had an inbuilt loyalty to my adoptive mother. She had done everything for me except give birth. It was quite a confusion in my mind. However, what developed naturally was that I slipped into calling my birth mother Bessie. She did not object, so that was the way it stayed. And my adoptive mother stays as Mummy or Mother, and I refer to her as my Durham mother.

In the second telephone call to Bessie, as she became from now on, I made it clear to her that I was going to come to Vancouver in the summer. Bessie did not object, which gave me the green light to go ahead and book my flights. It was not as simple as booking a flight and turning up in Vancouver with the hope that my mother would be there to meet me over a cup of coffee. Before spending a lot of money on the flights I needed to be sure that I would get some sort of welcome. Bessie hadn't convinced me that she would be pleased to see me. Once again, she promised to write and send photographs. I hadn't realised until I put the telephone down that it had been Mother's Day in Canada. In Britain, our Mother's Day is earlier in the year, in March. It never occurred to me that the two countries would have a different date. Throughout the call, she was still willing to talk to me. However, it was a little bit of a one-sided conversation. I wondered why the exchange appeared to be a bit guarded, but perhaps her other two daughters were within earshot. Or perhaps she was just embarrassed to speak to me on Mother's Day, thinking that I had telephoned knowing it was meant to be a special day.

I thought it would be a good idea to follow up the telephone call with a letter confirming that I would be booking my flight for July. My letter was another long eight-pager, as I wanted to tell Bessie a bit more about my life. She told me, during the telephone call, that she had cut her hand and damaged some tendons. I was particularly sympathetic as I had done something similar as a child. When I was eleven, I slipped and fell through a window. My left hand went through the glass, cutting three tendons and an artery in my wrist, just missing the main nerve. Blood seemed to be everywhere, covering walls, ceiling and floor. It was quite dramatic. I clasped my wrist tightly with my right hand to try and stem the flow of the blood and made my way to find my father. I knew my mother was not in the house. He promptly fainted. Fortunately, at that point, my mother walked in through the front door. She grabbed a tea towel from the kitchen and used it as a tourniquet prior to driving me to the hospital, which was less than ten minutes away. I was fast tracked into the operating theatre under the care of a plastic surgeon. Today my hand is normal, apart from an unsightly scar on my wrist. The only problem is the scar is in just the place where people might think I had made a suicide attempt. This has often led to some awkward conversations. I decided that it was important to get this story told to Bessie before we met. I did not want her seeing the resulting scar and worrying what might have gone wrong in my life.

Within the family we discussed my going to Canada. The debate centred around whether we should all go, whether Peter should come with me or whether I should go on my own. Peter had the notion it might create too much pressure on Bessie if he turned up, so the first meeting should be low key and as unthreatening as possible. I agreed with this, even though I would have liked us all to go. I was fine going on my own, but we thought it would be nice if Bridgette came with me. Girls together was unlikely to be too daunting a prospect for Bessie. After all, Bridgette was Bessie's granddaughter. I booked the flight for 20 July 1993. Bridgette would turn nineteen in the September and after the summer holidays she was due to go to university in London. The timing was perfect, giving her a break after studying for her A level examinations. The plan was that we would be in Vancouver for nine days, staying with Peter's cousin Michael and his wife Daphne. We would be able to visit Michael's father, Peter's Uncle Ivan. A close friend of mine, Sylvia, also lived in Vancouver, so I was looking forward to meeting up with her. Whatever happened with the reunion with Bessie, we would still have a good holiday.

In a further telephone call to Bessie, I told her the flights were booked, and Bridgette would be with me. She said she would be home and would meet us, but no concrete day was fixed. I had booked the flights seven weeks before we were due to travel, so there was plenty of time to finalise the details. But as the weeks went by and it got closer to our departure date, Bessie had still not contacted me. I wrote to her again reconfirming our flight times and where we would be staying. I said I would telephone to verify the final details. Again, I heard nothing from Bessie.

Chapter 21

My work at Huddersfield University had become intense. I was engrossed with assessments and exam boards. Also, much of my time was taken up rewriting all the textile design courses into accredited modular programmes. This had to be done by the September. It involved rewriting the BTEC, BA, BSc and MA courses. The governing body for universities appeared to revel in paperwork. Because I headed the BSc Textile course that had the largest number of students, I was the person in the department who had been given this demanding task. I had to put on hold any of my own design work, even though I had an agent in New York nagging me to send her my latest design samples.

I was staying in London, with work, the week before Bridgette and I were due to leave for Vancouver and there was still no word from Bessie. In London I hadn't much time to think about the trip because I was travelling with a group of final year textile design students. I had arranged for them to exhibit their work from their final year exhibition at the New Designers, a leading graduate design show at the Business Centre in Islington. It was Friday 16 July, only days before the flight to Canada. At that point it all seemed unreal. First it had been "a month to go", then "a week to go" and now it was "next Tuesday". Over the past weeks my mind had also been fully occupied with university validations and end of year design shows. I had little time to get excited about boarding the plane, with Bridgette, to Vancouver.

It was only two days before the flight and Bessie still hadn't answered or returned my calls. I thought it was strange. All I ever got was the answerphone. I knew one of her sisters, Nancy Broadchurch, lived in California, and I convinced myself she had taken flight and gone to the US so as not to face me, her daughter.

With a growing feeling of despondency, I thought I should cancel the trip as it was not going to work. But being just two days before Bridgette and I were due to travel, if I cancelled, I would lose the flight fares. So I thought I had no other choice but to go. I deduced that Bessie just did not want to face up to what had happened all those years ago. She must have been dreading me arriving and could not bring herself to say so. Overcoming my desperate disappointment, I concluded that Bridgette and I could still have a great holiday with Daphne and Michael, Peter's Uncle Ivan and I could see my friend Sylvia.

Vancouver is a wonderful picturesque coastal city in Western Canada, well worth a visit. There would be so much to see, with the backdrop of mountains, attractive city water inlets, modern shopping areas, Stanley Park, and the sea with many offshore islands. Bridgette and I agreed that we would still go and, just maybe, we could peek at Bessie's apartment. What had we to lose by turning a tough situation into an amazing holiday? Anyway, that is what I convinced myself, and I wanted Bridgette to have an enjoyable time.

It was 07:30 on Monday morning, 19 July. I planned to set off early for work at the university to tie up loose ends before Bridgette and I headed off to Vancouver the next day. I left the house, locked the back porch door, and descended one of the three steps with a view to making my way across the courtyard to the garage. Peter had gone to work, and Bridgette and James were still in bed. I could hear the telephone in the kitchen ringing. Being out of the house with the door locked and the key in my bag, my first thought was that I could not be bothered to go back and pick up the phone. But something made me change my mind and, reluctantly, I retraced my steps. Curiosity got the better of me as to who could be ringing at that time in the morning. I imagined what would happen was that as I made it back into the house, the person would hang up. However, the telephone kept ringing, and I managed to get there in time.

The voice I heard on the other end of the telephone was Bessie's. I was shocked and could not immediately work out the time difference between the UK and Vancouver. She told me it was half past eleven on the Sunday night and that she was on Vancouver Island seeing her daughters. She had, at last, summoned up the courage to tell my two half-sisters of my existence.

I was so relieved she had phoned. It had taken her a year of agonising since I first established a presence in her life, which started with the Edmonton Journal cutting on 11 September 1992. She was worried about how her two Canadian daughters would react to the news of her first-born child. All along this had been the obstacle in relation to contacting me for fear of losing them. I found it sad that she felt it was either me or them and somehow, thought she could not have both. I'm sure her fears were typical of many mothers trying to come to terms with a reunion, where there had been years of concealment from their later children.

Later, my sisters told me the full story behind Bessie telling them of my arrival, both into this world and then in Vancouver. Bessie hadn't gone to stay with her sister in California as I had feared. All the time she was at home in a state of anxiety.

It was usual for Bessie to go and stay, for a few days over a weekend, with each of my sisters on Vancouver Island. Patricia, who I got to know as Trish, was born in 1952, and my younger sister Gail in 1956.

It was just days before Bridgette and I were due to travel, when Gail said her mother came over to Vancouver Island to stay. Bessie seemed nervous and distracted. This was unusual for her and out of character. It was the Sunday evening and after Gail's two boys, then aged two and five, were in bed, her mother said she had something that she wanted to talk about. Gail was worried and immediately asked her if she was ill or even worse, dying. After her mother replied "no" to both these questions, Gail then felt distinctly more relaxed. Whatever her mother had to say could not be worse than being seriously ill.

Trish continued with the story. She said her mother was staying at Gail's and they called and asked her to come over, which was not out of the ordinary. When Trish arrived, she was puzzled why her mother appeared so distressed and anxious.

After a bit of coaxing, Bessie then came straight out with the truth that she had had a baby during the war who had been adopted in England. To Bessie's surprise, Trish replied saying that she had known about me all along. Trish recalled how I was the centre of a conversation that her parents had before they were divorced. At about the age of ten she sat quietly on the stairs, when she should have been in bed, and had inadvertently overheard a discussion between her parents referring to a baby. Trish had at some point told Gail, but it was not something Gail had thought about in recent times. Gail had it in her mind that I was a boy.

Most of the family had been aware of my existence for at least twenty-five years. It was my mother who was shocked that her daughters knew about another older sibling. The family had treated it as a taboo subject and my birth was never mentioned. Who spilt the beans first was a bit of a mystery, and there were various stories in the family about who was the original teller of the tale.

Years ago, after Trish had overheard her parents talking about me, she contacted her friend Elaine whose mother, Marg, was in the RCAF with Bessie in London. Marg was one of Bessie's closest friends who knew about the pregnancy. At Trish's bidding, Elaine had asked her mother if Bessie had a baby during the war. Marg, thinking that Bessie had told Trish, confirmed that I was born in England in 1945. Trish never felt comfortable asking her mother about me. It became the secret that nobody spoke about, but everyone individually knew.

On that Sunday evening at Gail's, it was the girls' turn to be shocked when Bessie told them, "Well what you don't know is that your eldest sister is arriving in Vancouver on Tuesday." My sisters were then worried that I was about to board the plane with no one to welcome me when I landed.

As I was speaking to Bessie on the telephone, Trish took the receiver from our mother to speak to me. I told her I was hugely relieved to get the call and to make contact. I said I had visions of Bridgette and me walking around their hometown "incognito". Trish reassured me there would be no chance of that happening as they were excited at the thought of meeting the two of us.

Trish said she was desperate to telephone me the minute Bessie had poured out the truth about my existence. She was aware of the time difference to Britain and did not want to telephone in the middle of the night. They stayed up late until they knew they could make the call at a sociable time when they thought I would be getting up for the day. British Columbia is eight hours behind the UK.

It was so sad that Bessie did not have the conversation with her daughters about me decades ago. By doing so, she might have unburdened her guilt and relieved some of the stress that had become ingrained throughout her life. Her shame became so entrenched and was buried so deeply, that she found it impossible to disclose her secret, even though she was now in her early seventies. For Bessie, having an illegitimate baby had developed into a massive obstacle. She worried how her girls and the rest of the family would judge her if her secret ever got out.

Even as a young girl, Trish had occasionally wondered about me. When Gail first heard mention of me from Trish, she had been too young to work out the issues related to a wartime baby. Trish told me she had intended to search for me at some point, even though she knew she could not ask her mother for any information. In her mind it seemed a tricky situation and she wondered if it might be a scenario that played out in their mother's final moments.

After I put the telephone down early that Monday morning, I was thrilled that at last there had been some proper contact. Even better, my two sisters were equally excited about meeting Bridgette and me. It was wonderful, after all these months and years of hoping and searching, that knowledge of my existence with my family in Canada was now valid. I basked in the pleasure of appreciating that my own birth mother had at last opened to the whole truth. I drove the nineteen miles to the university at Huddersfield feeling I needed to tell the world. I was bursting to break the news to everyone. It was more difficult spreading the word to my friends in those days, as there were few mobile telephones. Sending a quick text or making a hands-free call from the car was not an option.

But before leaving the house, I phoned Peter to relate the story. We then thought we wished we were all going to Vancouver as a family. My colleagues at work knew all about my pending visit to meet my birth mother, but I hadn't shared the fact that Bessie had made no contact with me. I could now genuinely tell them that she and my sisters were looking forward to my arrival in Canada.

Chapter 22

E arly in the morning of Tuesday 20 July 1993, Bridgette and I flew from Manchester airport to Canada. We changed flights in Toronto with a tight turnaround. Not even time for a cup of coffee. Once back in the air, we were on our way to Vancouver. Looking down from the cloudless sky, it struck me what a large flat place most of the central southern plains of Canada appeared to be. It was strange seeing Lake Superior, like a large ocean, spread out below me. Geography was one subject that I liked at school, and I learnt how to remember the Great Lakes with the mnemonic "Some Men Hate Eating Oranges": Superior, Michigan, Huron, Erie, and Ontario. Here I was peering down on this far away, inland freshwater lake and then the prairies that I'd studied at school. Taking in the landscape's physical features, with clear skies and good visibility, was like turning the pages of a familiar map.

The flight followed the border between the US and Canada across Manitoba, Saskatchewan, Alberta and finally to British Columbia. As Bridgette and I gazed out of the window, we were amazed at the enormous farmlands that spread out for what looked like a thousand miles. We would glance out of the window, then fall asleep, wake up and peer out again to see the same scenery which never appeared to change. There were huge flat fields and little habitation. Bridgette was better at sleeping than I was. Even as a tiny baby she could sleep anywhere at any time, just like her father. In her highchair, suddenly, she would be fast asleep with her head in her food. I was awake most of the journey, enjoying the experience but apprehensive about how I was going to cope when we landed.

The Rocky Mountains then dramatically came into view, rising high up from the flat farmlands. The Rockies landscape was staggering with its glaciers, lakes, snow-capped mountains and dense forest areas. After the Rockies, and nearing our destination, we flew over the coastal mountain range that overlooked Vancouver. As we started to descend to the airport, a thick layer of low cloud ruined our view. This thick cloud cover remained for most of our visit, not letting Bridgette and me appreciate the wider beauty of the city and its setting. We landed early evening. With the eight-hour time difference in British Columbia, it was after midnight at home and Peter and James would be in bed. It was even later before we got through customs and collected our bags. We had decided in advance that I would telephone home the next day.

Daphne and Michael were waiting at the barrier for us to emerge from customs. They were welcoming and pleased to see us.

We drove through the city for just under an hour to reach their house in West Vancouver. They lived in a beautiful affluent residential area, near to a golf club called Gleneagles. The houses were built into a steep rocky hillside with sea views. It was located between the Burrard Inlet and the main road north to Whistler known as Highway 99. The area was renowned for its parks and tall evergreen cypress trees. The picturesque district was overlooked by mountains.

Daphne and Michael's three sons, just a little older than Bridgette, were at home to greet us, as well as their two Dachshund dogs, Twopence and Schulz. Bridgette slept outside in the cutest little summer house which doubled up as Daphne's pottery studio. The one thing Bridgette was not prepared for was the nocturnal raccoons, which she could hear trying to scavenge in the waste bins. The raccoons were clever, they would tip over a bin to rummage in its content. Bins had to be securely fastened down with a lockable tight lid. It was comfortable staying with Peter's cousin, who was someone I had known since I was eighteen. It made me feel less vulnerable. Having Bridgette with me helped to keep me grounded and created a distraction from getting too nervous about meeting my birth mother.

The next morning Daphne drove Bridgette and me to Bessie's apartment for the prearranged time of eleven o'clock. We arrived exactly on time. As Daphne drew up outside, I saw what looked like a small apartment block. Daphne explained it was a condominium, run by a Condominium Co-operative. I could not get the hang of what that meant though I gathered that Bessie was in a government housing scheme for the elderly. It was a tidy clean-cut square concrete-looking building, rendered and painted donkey grey. It sat on a corner site and looked as if there would be about ten apartments within the block. Bridgette and I got out of Daphne's sturdy four-wheeled drive, Sport Utility Vehicle, with me feeling more than a little apprehensive. I persuaded Daphne to come inside with us to meet my mother. I was relieved when she agreed, as I needed some support.

We went up the short path and rang the bell next to Bessie's name. As Bessie opened the door, I could see that she was not tall. She wore a cobalt blue, short sleeved round necked blouse, with matching-coloured casual trousers. There was a thin gold chain round her neck with a charm or locket which I could not make out. Her smile was warm which was enhanced by her dimples. There was a significant gap in her front teeth, which I found out later was a Hamilton family trait. I have a gap between my front two teeth, but not as prominent. It was a strange coincidence, as my Durham mother also had a large gap between her front two teeth. My mother was always proud of this gap and could get a thick coin between her teeth which she said was good luck and a sign of wealth. Not being superstitious, I did not believe in this theory, but it was a strange coincidence that we all had the same feature. Not only did my two mothers share the Hamilton name but they also had the gap. Bessie's hair was short, softly permed, and dyed blonde about the same colour as mine. It was obvious that Bessie was as nervous as I was. On meeting, we just said hello without any physical contact.

I was pleased to have Daphne with me to start up an informal line of chat. To begin with, Bessie and I did not know what to say to each other. Bessie's wartime friend Mary was sitting at the table. Clearly, Bessie also needed support as she felt she could not handle the situation on her own. Mary was a petite, pretty woman, even in her advancing years. With Daphne and Mary helping to break the ice, the atmosphere became easier. I was surprised when Daphne, after finishing her coffee, said "bye, see you later". I was willing her not to go and leave Bridgette and me to manage on our own. But of course, what else could Daphne do? She could not sit in on what was meant to be a private moment between mother, daughter, and granddaughter. With mother and daughter seeing each other for the first time in forty-eight years.

I was not sure if Bessie had any preconceived ideas as to what I might be like. I had certainly pushed any thoughts of her life and appearance well to the back of my mind. I genuinely wanted to accept her for who she was. Those romantic thoughts of a ten-year-old girl were left far behind. I just hoped she was not feeling too threatened by my arrival. However, if she was, she showed little sign of it.

We settled into an easy conversation, helped by looking at old photographs. I kept wanting to stare at Bessie so that I could take in all her features. I was trying to do this surreptitiously without being rude and it made me wonder if she was doing the same. She told me she was five foot four inches, a little shorter than me. Her blood type was "O" rhesus negative, the same as mine. Her hands were square shaped like mine, and she was big boned as I was. Not overweight at all but not skinny. Our eyes were similar, and she had dimples, which Bridgette and I have both inherited. The one thing I did notice was her feet, given that she was wearing sandals, and I could see her toes. They were large with a long, big toe, again like mine. I found it strange to think that half my genetic make-up came from this woman sitting opposite me, across the small table just big enough for four or five people to sit round. Here I was looking at my mother for the first time in my living memory. When being bought up from a baby by your natural mother, the familiarity would mean that questions of likeness would be taken for granted. Now I was seeing the person who brought me into the world all those years ago.

When I had first entered the apartment, I noticed a photograph, sitting inside an A4 frame on a sideboard. It was of a young woman of about Bridgette's age and the resemblance to my daughter was uncanny. I nearly burst out saying, "how did you get this photograph of Bridgette?" but then common sense took a grip, and I asked nonchalantly who the girl in the picture was. It turned out to be my youngest half-sister Gail, taken when she would have been about eighteen. The likeness to Bridgette was remarkable.

After Daphne left, we went through the copies of my adoption file that I had brought for Bessie to see. I could not pluck up enough courage to ask about my father and decided to leave that for another day. In the brief time we had been talking, I knew that I liked this person who was my mother. She was sociable with a sense of fun and mischief. I must be honest and say that, although I became perfectly comfortable in her company, I did not experience a great immediate blood bond. I found it hard to imagine that Bessie had given birth to me. After an hour or so, Bessie's elder sister, my Aunt Sal, arrived, and Mary left. Sal was taller than my mother, being slim with dyed mousy brown hair, covering any grey. She appeared active and organised and genuinely seemed pleased to meet Bridgette and me.

It was decided that Sal would drive us round and show her newfound relatives the sights of Vancouver. I was uneasy with calling her aunt for the first time at the age of forty-eight, so the name Sal stuck. First, we had lunch at a restaurant chain called White Spot. White Spot had originated in Vancouver and was known for its freshly made hamburgers and milkshakes. I was expecting something like a McDonald's and had no expectation that the food would be good. So Bridgette and I were pleasantly surprised because White Spot was enjoyable with excellent fresh food. What we were not prepared for was the waiter service. As in most of Canada, waiters instantly become your best friend, bombarding you with endless inane chat, wanting to know everything you had been doing that day. This was quite a contrast from the UK, where waiters are far more subdued. On balance, I found the British way preferable. Canadian waiters are not well paid, and they are desperate for healthy tips. But how could I say what I was doing that day – "out for lunch with my mother who I hadn't met since I was born". I really did not want to be talking to the White Spot staff about my day.

After lunch, we went to the Queen Elizabeth Park, a beautifully landscaped quarry garden with an arboretum, an area devoted to trees and shrubs. It was on high ground with spectacular views over the city, looking across to the mountain ranges and towards where Daphne and Michael lived. In the park was a sculpture by

Henry Moore. It was a large bronze, instantly recognisable, known as the Knife Edge Two Piece. Henry Moore was born in Castleford in 1898, nine miles from our home in Wakefield. On the outskirts of Wakefield is the Yorkshire Sculpture Park, home to the largest collection of Henry Moore's enormous bronze sculptures. Seeing the sculpture made me feel that this was not such a foreign country after all. However, I knew more about Henry Moore than many Canadians.

There was no chance of dawdling in the garden as the weather was not good. It was still damp with a low mist set in for the day, which was a shame as the views were not as great as they should have been. We posed for photographs with each other, then it was decided to move on to a more sheltered location.

To my great surprise, the sheltered location was to be a bingo hall. To be more precise, a brand new, swish, modern computerised bingo hall. I had to come clean and say that I knew nothing about bingo. I had never played the game in my life and Bridgette hadn't either. After all, I was brought up by a vicar and gambling was seen to be sinful. Bessie and Sal interpreted my comment as never having played "computerised bingo". They could make no sense of the possibility that I might never have played any sort of bingo before. The time we spent playing bingo was a bit of a haze in my mind, as I had no clue what I was doing. Even if I had won, I would not have known what was going on. I do remember it being a bit of fun and it was good to do something different. Also, whilst in Vancouver, Bessie introduced me to Lotto, and I bought my first ever ticket for the Canadian 6/49 Lottery. This was 1993 and the British Lottery was not launched until a year later. It was exciting to check out my ticket, but of course, I won nothing. I continue to win nothing on our British Lotto, so what about the gaps in our teeth that is meant to signify wealth?

Sal drove Bridgette and me back to Daphne and Michael's house in West Vancouver. On the way, before going over the Lions Gate suspension bridge, which crosses the Burrard Inlet connecting North and West Vancouver to the City, we had a tour of Stanley Park. The bridge is unusual as it has three reversible lane signals that can swap around to accommodate the heaviest direction of traffic. The park is on a peninsular sticking out from the west end of the city. This is an amazing place, opened in 1888 by Lord Stanley, who was the then Governor of Vancouver. The park is about 1,000 acres of dense forest and close to downtown Vancouver. My lasting memory was of the tall Douglas firs and the large Red Cedar trees. Our favourite was the collection of Totem Poles made by the indigenous people. We had never seen an authentic Totem Pole before. They are carved and painted so beautifully with a height of anything from three to eighteen metres. Of course, more photographs were taken.

Bessie and Sal came into Daphne and Michael's house, just to say "hello" and to plan for the next day. After Sal and Bessie left, I discussed the day with Peter's cousin. By the evening, Bridgette and I were shattered, both physically and mentally, and were pleased to go to bed. Bridgette left for her little summer house, and I went to the guest room. I was so glad to have Bridgette with me, and to have Daphne and Michael to come home to at the end of a surprising day. That night, I did not allow myself to dwell too much on how I felt about meeting a second mother. I was not going to be too analytical so early in our physical relationship, and anyway, I needed to empty my mind and sleep. It was not the right time to scrutinise my emotions. I had assumed a polite approach towards Bessie, as anyone would, having met, to all intents and purposes, a stranger for the first time.

Chapter 23

The next morning, Michael dropped Bridgette and me off in downtown Vancouver, where we met Bessie. We wandered around, looking at shops in the city and then we caught the Sky Train to New Westminster. I found out later that the attraction of New Westminster was a casino. I later realised it was where Bessie really wanted to take us. Following our reaction to the computer bingo, she may have been a bit cautious about mentioning a casino. For many people, low key gambling such as slot machines, appeared to be extremely popular in British Columbia. There are huge halls with banks of slot machines; it's seen as a perfectly normal recreational pursuit.

In the shops, I noticed all the clothes were manufactured from synthetic fibres, while most of the clothes I wore were made from natural fibres. The 1990s Canadian relaxed styles were quite different from home. Even in the city, men went to work in shorts and women in casual gear. While wandering through a department store Bessie wanted to buy me an outfit. She was wanting to dress me in an outfit that was familiar to her. Was it her way of claiming back her daughter? Our day was good, and we had Bessie to ourselves with her seeming to be perfectly comfortable and enjoying showing us the city. We did a lot of walking, which did not faze her at all. For her age, in her early seventies, Bessie appeared remarkably fit.

After a full day out, Bridgette and I got the bus back to Daphne and Michael's. The day was a new experience for us both, we were used to European cities which were unlike Vancouver in so many ways. The west of Canada is a cleaner and historically much younger place than anywhere in Europe, it does not have the ancestry and broader culture of Britain. It was the scenery and not the buildings that caught my eye. It's the most panoramic breathtaking city I had ever visited, even in the mist and rain. But it felt foreign, like in another world. The relaxed behaviour, the way of life, the food, the tastes and interests seemed so far away from my upbringing in the Northeast of England. As a holiday destination it was perfect, but it was strange trying to imagine that this place could have been my home. I know I would have been happy in Vancouver, but what I could not work out in my head was, what kind of person I would have been and what my personality might have been like. I would never have met Peter and hence my children would have been different. Now that did feel weird as my children are simply perfect as they are. All I could think of was my love for my Durham mother and the city where I grew up. I needed time to form a bond with Bessie and to come to terms with the nature of my love for two mothers. It was still too early to structure any conclusions, and I realised that I would have to give it much more time. I certainly felt the pressure of the enormity of the event that I had set in motion. It was easier for Bessie as she was on her home ground, while I was coping with new relationships as well as being in a strange environment.

The next day my two half-sisters, Trish and Gail, came over from Vancouver Island to pick Bridgette and me up from Daphne and Michael's. They had taken the hour and a half ferry ride from Nanaimo to Horseshoe Bay across the Strait of Georgia. I instantly liked Trish and Gail and felt relaxed in their company.

I was able to relate to them much better than I imagined, even though I was nervous and worried about meeting them. I had no idea how they would react to this older sister turning up. I need not have had any fears, though, because they were relaxed, and the conversation was easy.

We visited Granville Market, famous for its farmers' retail outlet and brewing company. Granville Island is a peninsula formed by a sandbar jutting out into False Creek. False Creek is a short blind water inlet in the heart of Vancouver. Traditionally the island was used by the indigenous people as a fishing area. Then it had been an old industrial manufacturing site but now it housed an excellent food market, shops and restaurants. There were masses of house boats and yachts moored around False Creek, making it a picturesque place to be. It became my favourite spot in Vancouver.

The plan was that my two sisters would stay the night with Bessie. Then the next day they were to collect Bridgette and me to set off to spend two nights on Vancouver Island. In British terms, Vancouver Island is large for an island. It's 283 miles in length and 62 miles wide at its broadest point. It has a population of just under nine hundred thousand, just a bit more than the metro area of Newcastle upon Tyne. Bridgette and I stayed with Trish, while Bessie was at Gail's house.

Trish and Gail were both slightly smaller in height than me. Trish had curly brown hair, and Gail was fair with her hair tied back in a short ponytail. Gail's two sons and Trish's two daughters were all younger than Bridgette and James. Trish's eldest daughter Carrie, coincidentally, had the same birth date as Stuart, although she was five years younger. Both my sisters' husbands were easy going, taking in their stride the new additions to the family.

We loved Vancouver Island and on the one full day we were there, we visited the sandy beaches and swam in the sea. It was a relaxing time, and I began to feel I could dare to start thinking about my impression of my newfound family. During all this period I kept a diary, just as I have periodically, throughout my life, especially when times became difficult. I need to write my thoughts down to make sense of the mental picture.

I realised I was putting up a subconscious barrier which was stopping me from accepting Bessie for who she was. In a strange way, I was trying to mould her into who I wanted her to be. What had been happening was that I had been expecting Bessie to be like my Durham mother. At every move, I was comparing the two mothers instead of accepting them as two separate people. I was trying to bring back the mother I had loved and known all my life and who was now dead. I was wanting to rekindle the mother who had bought me up. All the time in my mind, I was assessing one mother against the other. Of course, this was hugely unfair on Bessie, because by doing this, she would always be disadvantaged. I needed to separate out in my head that they were two distinct individuals with their own different personalities.

As soon as I sorted this out in my head, my whole attitude changed towards Bessie. I saw her for what she was and recognised all her strengths. It did not matter that there was no immediate feeling of a maternal bond. I enjoyed being in her company and was fascinated by her life and the beautiful city where she lived. It was easier for Bridgette, as her grandmother in England had died when she was only eight. After Bridgette was born, we did not live near Durham, so she did not have much opportunity to get close to her maternal grandmother. Bridgette took it all in her stride and settled into having a good holiday. Although she did have to endure quite a bit of sitting around listening to "adult" boring chat. Nonetheless, she was comfortable with everything that was going on.

On meeting Bessie and her sister, my aunt Sal, I was quite relieved that they were not overemotional and gushing. I would not have felt comfortable meeting someone who threw their arms around me and started crying. Bessie was not outwardly sentimental, as neither was my Durham mother. I was bought up not to show my feelings in grand displays. This was how both my mothers were and, frankly, I was quite thankful for that. Their common link was that their thoughts and feelings were concealed and not always evidently expressed.

The next day we said our goodbyes to Trish and Gail. Bessie, Bridgette and I got the hour and a half ferry back to Vancouver. I knew I would see them again even though we lived almost 5,000 miles apart. On the ferry, it seemed a perfect opportunity to ask Bessie about my father. I was not going to get another opportunity to be quietly alone with her. Bridgette was happily exploring the boat and looking in the shop. Bessie told me that he was from Ontario and was in the RCAF. He was with Bomber Command as a mid-gunner on a Halifax bomber based in Yorkshire. The crew often came to London when they were on leave. Her best friend Marg was seeing another crew member. They would go to pubs, like The Roebuck, in the West End.

When Bessie became pregnant, her relationship with my father ended. She told me that she saw him a couple of times after I was born. He had asked if she was OK as he had known there was a baby. But by then he had a new girlfriend who was an English girl from London. She said that my father and her did not have a lot in common and it was a bit of a "hit and miss" affair.

Bessie said she had first met my father in Halifax, Nova Scotia when their transport ship was leaving for Britain in July 1944. After that, I was not able to get much more out of her. I was reluctant to press her more for fear of upsetting the relationship that we were beginning to form.

The ferry trip was picturesque as there was, at last, a change in the weather. We had sunshine and blue skies. The journey from Nanaimo to Horseshoe Bay was impressive. Passing by numerous gulf islands and seeing the extensive coastal range of mountains on the mainland was quite breath-taking. It must be one of the most beautiful ferry rides in the world.

Bridgette and I returned to Daphne and Michael's house. There were only a couple of nights left before catching the flight home. I managed to squeeze in a short visit to see my friend Sylvia, who had emigrated to Vancouver from Newcastle upon Tyne over twenty years earlier. I had known Sylvia when I was eighteen as she was the elder sister of my close friend and nursing colleague, Linda.

The time we had left before our return was hectic. The next day was spent meeting many of Bessie's friends and she seemed keen to show me off. However, without any warning to me, she introduced me as a friend's daughter who she had met during the war when she was in London. Sometimes she would say I was "a sort of relative". She seemed reluctant to own up that I was her daughter. I found that a little strange but understandable – she hadn't yet had time to think through exactly how she felt about her new-found child, or how she would explain the circumstances of my birth. At this point, I was happy to go along with this explanation of my visit to Vancouver.

We met Bessie's close friends at her favourite haunt, the Billy Bishop Legion Club, which was within walking distance of her apartment. We also met her recent boyfriend, Les, who was slightly younger than her. Les, I thought, was an unusual companion as he lived on a houseboat which was not seaworthy. The boat did manage to float as it was moored up in the Creek near to Bessie's apartment. Bessie was enjoying herself and was in an intimate relationship with him. He had a massive dog who took up all the space in the back of his car. Who was I to judge her personal love life? As Bessie was seventy-one, it hadn't occurred to me that she might share a bed with a comparatively new man friend.

My mother was a devotee of the Legion Club in Vancouver, a busy, lively place of fun and friendship for many ex-military people. The club was named after Willian Avery Bishop. He was a legendary First World War RAF pilot who was honoured with many distinguished medals such as the Victoria Cross and the Military Cross. Bessie was proud of the club and spent a lot of her time there. She was the first female President of the Vancouver Legion which was originally set up in 1945, to support active and veteran Air Force personnel. The membership is currently extended to veterans of all the services and their visitors. Bridgette and I were made extremely welcome.

My Aunt Sal and Bessie's wartime friend Mary joined us in the Billy Bishop. We also met two of my cousins, who were amiable and friendly. Nobody could have made us feel more welcome. Bessie had arranged a "party" meal at her apartment. It was not only a welcome gathering but also a goodbye get-together as we had just one more day before flying home. Mary talked to me a lot about the war, but she hadn't known my father, unlike Bessie's other friend Marg. Marg lived further north, in a place called Kamloops in British Columbia. Marg's daughter Elaine was the close friend of Trish, who Trish had asked about my birth in England. Mary did confide to me that Bessie was offered the chance to have me aborted but she refused. She told me that Bessie was quite happy during her pregnancy and that she stoically faced the prospect that after I was born and adopted, she would never see me again.

The one thing I did discover about Bessie was that she was musical. Not anything like my Durham mother, as Bessie had had no formal music tuition. But she had rhythm and a natural memory for tunes. Bessie was drawn to the opposite genre of music to my Durham mother in that she loved 1920s swing bands and jazz. I was surprised when she told me that she always carried a pair of spoons in her bag. At every opportunity, she got them out and clicked them rhythmically to any music with a beat that happened to be playing. She was extremely good and tried to teach me to play. It was fun and to this day I still have the pair of her spoons that she kept in her handbag. I must admit these spoons are nothing special, just two old kitchen spoons, but they were the ones she used, and I treasure them. One mother was a professional classical violin musician, and the other was an experienced and talented spoon player. Quite a contrast in musical styles, but it summed up the strange but similar differences between my two mothers.

Bridgette and I spent the last day with Daphne and Michael. We had planned an easy day, getting up late, chatting and going out for a meal at a place called The Keg at Horseshoe Bay. During the day, Trish telephoned, as did Bessie. Throughout our stay in Vancouver, the weather was awful with only two good days in total. It had been their worst summer for twenty years.

We were up and packed by 04:30 the next morning for our flight home. Daphne and Michael dropped us at the airport, and we were grateful that they had been so kind as well as being lots of fun. Michael's exuberant personality never allowed for a melancholy moment and there was always a funny remark to keep Bridgette and me going through what could have potentially been a difficult week.

Bessie and Les also came to the airport, and we had a farewell breakfast with them before we went through the security checks to board the plane. Before leaving, Bessie gave us presents for the family. There was a little one for each of us, including Peter and James, with a personal note attached. My note said, "It was great meeting you. I'm so happy you found me and that you were able to make the trip." This could be interpreted in no other way than it was my birth mother stretching out a virtual hug of motherly love. If she was not demonstrative with any physical hugs, I certainly got a big one with that note.

As we boarded the plane, I wondered if I would see Vancouver again. On the other hand, I knew I would see Bessie and Trish and Gail in the future as the bond had been cemented. The last nine days had been more than just a fascinating experience and not in the least how I imagined it would have been. What an amazing and exceptional welcome we had, with everyone we met completely accepting us without judgment. This warmth almost made me more confused as to who I was. I had thought we would have met Bessie a couple of times over a cup of tea in the classical British way, but it was so much more. It had been a full-scale embrace, right into the very heart of my new family.

I was dying to talk it through with Peter. I could not wait to get home to him and James. And Bridgette and I were longing to get back to our own beds. For most of the time, Bridgette had been sleeping in an up-market garden shed. She had enjoyed the space and the comfort it provided. Even though there was a sadness at leaving my birth mother and my half-sisters and the beautiful city of Vancouver, it would be good to return to normality. As the weeks went by, questions kept buzzing round in my head. There was so much more to take in. Where was my trip likely to lead me? Was I going to travel further down the road of learning a bit more about my father? Would I cement a stronger relationship with both my half-sisters and when would I be compelled to return? What was it like for Bessie during wartime Britain? Would she ever be likely to introduce me as her new-found daughter to her friends in the Billy Bishop Legion Club? Would any of my new family ever visit Britain? And, finally, had I managed to make much real progress in coming to terms with the feeling of dislocation? The idea of being brought up by one family whilst inherently, in some senses, belonging to another family was confusing. Yet did it, or should it, really matter?

Part 5:

—

Shed the Guilt and Bury the Blame

Chapter 24

I t was a glorious holiday in Canada meeting for the first time my birth family and many of Bessie's friends. But this was never really intended as a holiday. The main purpose was to meet my birth mother for the first time, or if you count my birth, it was for the second time in my life. By calling it a holiday I was protecting myself in case Bessie was unable to come to terms with accepting me as her daughter. What I did experience was a wonderful welcome with a real sense of belonging. I became one of the family and my mother appeared to be just as proud of her new-found daughter and granddaughter as she was of my two half-siblings. So, why was the question of "who am I?" still causing confusion in my mind? I was bought up in England by caring but "stiff upper lip" English parents, and I attended a typical English boarding school. In comparison any life I might have had in Canada would have been vastly different.

After just over a week, I had to leave British Columbia and return to my familiar life in England. I was left trying to work out how I truly felt about the person who gave birth to me. This was not as simple as I thought it would be. How to explain my life to Bessie in such a brief time with so many people around, was impossible and at times a little frustrating. I still felt she was not ready to delve into the emotional side of how she felt about the issues surrounding my birth. In her eyes, it may have been sufficient and simpler to start our relationship as if we had merely met as adults. Any actual reference to my birth and its aftermath seemed to be a bit premature for her. However, I got the impression that she may have felt some release from the deep anxiety she had been holding onto by never being able to mention her eldest daughter. At last, she had met her long-lost child. What guilt there might have been, and all the pretence in her life, was now over within her family if not with her friends. Hopefully, she would manage to reconcile that within her mind soon.

How hard it must have been, for Bessie, to remain silent to her parents, her siblings and most of all to her two later children. The terrible anxiety of being found to be living a lie must have been an unbearable burden. On a day-to-day basis Bessie had no one with whom she could share, what she perceived to be her shame. I was never going to challenge her or make her feel uncomfortable about giving me up for adoption. That was not in my personality. I felt nothing but compassion for her and the trauma she must have endured during my birth. It's a pity that I was never able to talk to my Durham mother about what it was like not being able to conceive children. I'm sure she felt intense sadness because of her infertility.

For the first few weeks after I arrived home from Vancouver, everyone I knew wanted to hear all the details of my story. They asked what it was like meeting Bessie, and how I felt. I found it difficult to answer some of their questions because it was hard to deal with my own thoughts as to how I felt about the situation. Talking about the practical things, such as the flight and the scenery was easy. The emotional side was more difficult, and I avoided getting into that part of the conversation. It occurred to me that I was making excuses to myself by thinking I was too busy to find a quiet moment to analyse the enormity of what had just taken place in Vancouver. Or was it just too hard to understand the depth of emotion within myself? Perhaps I was overcomplicating the issue and the consequences of my birth.

There was no doubt it was a wonderful whirlwind nine days that gave me a nice comforting feeling of satisfaction knowing that, at last, I had met my birth mother and my two half-sisters. On the other hand, it disturbed me slightly, as I was not prepared for the split loyalties that I felt towards my two mothers. I was now uncertain as to which mother could be regarded as my 'real' mother. Coming to terms with two mothers was far from easy. After all, I could love my three children equally, along with their differing contrasting personalities, so why not two mothers and accept their dissimilarities? I suppose this line of argument could be expanded to include the love for more than one partner, as many do. It made me wonder how foster children feel having a range of "mothers" as they move through various homes. It must be hard for them to work out their identities and to develop their own settled personalities.

I found in Bessie, who in many ways was different from my Durham mother, yet there were some similarities. One liked a drink, parties, and the social life around fruit machines in a casino and the Billy Bishop Legion Club, whilst the other was reserved and more comfortable in small social groups. One was a city girl, enjoyed male company and sport, whilst the other preferred being with her goats and Siamese cats and playing her violin. The things they had in common were that they were both motivated and committed to whatever they did. They were industrious, career-minded feminists and strongly independent. Although I hadn't known Bessie long, I quickly picked up that she was like my Durham mother in the way that she did not outwardly show her emotions. They were both good at covering up and coping when things were going wrong in their lives. They would never complain despite their adversities. They were pragmatic and got on with whatever they were presented with in life. Although Bessie liked men's company she certainly, like my Durham mother, would not defer to any man or be subservient.

I found myself thinking what it would have been like if the three of us, Bessie, my adopted mother, and I had met over a cup of coffee. I imagine the three of us sitting at our large kitchen table in the house in Durham and wonder how the conversation would have gone. I hope we would have agreed that the welfare of the child is paramount. But would we have discussed the feelings of a birth mother and an adoptive mother. How do they feel? It's easy to picture how horrific it is to give a child up at birth. But how is it for the birth mother years later when confronted with her child arriving back in her life? What about the adoptive mother who has invested her love for a child that is not her own? Where does that leave her when the child decides to break away to find their birth family? It's a triangle with three points, all equally as important to each other. One without the other would not hold the glue of the triangle together. The birth mother should not pretend that she hadn't given birth to a baby. The adoptive mother, although loving the child as her own, must not lose sight of the child's need to know her birth heritage however unsavoury to society that might be. The child, in most circumstances, needs to know their birth identity from an early age. The adoptive mother should be praised and supported for taking on what could potentially be an extremely demanding situation.

The three of us sitting around the kitchen table might not have been easy. Would it have worked? Could I have explained to them that I'm not sure where I belong with only one foot in each family door? My gut feeling is that the three of us meeting together might not have been beneficial. It could be that the many skeletons which were so deeply buried and the pain on all sides was too much to confront. Especially if the circumstances of birth were the consequence of incest or rape. I regard myself as one of the lucky adoptees.

The question of one's own identity may not be troubling to anybody who has had a standard upbringing with regular parentage. It was a question that kept cropping up in my mind as I tried to reconcile my recently discovered birth mother alongside the mother who had brought me up. My immediate conclusions were that I was a healthy mix of the two. A bit of an amalgamation of both. I'm reasonably adaptable and I can comfortably alter my behaviour to fit into any social situation. Peter would say I had traits of Bessie as I was certainly a party girl when I first met him. But I would say my tastes and attitudes to life were much like my Durham mother.

One of Bessie's loves was tap-dancing. Trish joked that I had a lucky escape as she was made to endure dancing lessons as a young child. She said it would have helped her if I had been around in the family, because as the eldest daughter, I would have been the one made to go to the tap-dancing classes. I know I would have been terrible at it, just as I was terrible in my ballet lessons that I attempted as a young child.

I summed up my dilemma by considering a simple question as to whether I would have followed the violin or the spoons. Have I the qualities of my Durham mother or the characteristics of Bessie? Perhaps a bit of both.

I do prefer the countryside to the city, yet, now and then, I must have some exposure to the bustle of city life just like Bessie.

I love nice clothes, I love the theatre, I love European culture, I love Georgian architecture and visiting museums and galleries, like many of the things my Durham mother was passionate about.

This got me pondering about nature versus nurture and trying to figure out where my personality cross-matched with my ancestry. This question did occupy a lot of my thinking. Then I wondered if the question of nature versus nurture arises in most people's minds or is it in the thoughts of those separated from their biological parents? During the weeks after I returned from Canada, I was in a better position to judge who I resembled most closely, my Durham mother or Bessie. It was a question that was about working out the patterns of one's personality and which bits are given naturally through genes, and which came from one's path through life.

I wanted some clarity, for my own satisfaction, as to which abilities and characteristics I thought I might have acquired from being English or which came from my Canadian birth mother. I began to feel a bit guilty by almost placing my two mothers into unconscious competition. I had to tell myself to relax and just be my own person as I was starting to overcomplicate the debate around my genes and life experiences. All this worrying throughout my life about "who am I?" was becoming counterproductive. I had reached a point of wanting to settle into simply being me, and meeting Bessie gave me permission to do just that. Although, I did conclude that I don't believe there is a simple split between nature and nurture. For me I have settled into a three-way split. One part, thirty percent, I decided was inevitably my genetic makeup. The rest, I maintain, is divided equally between the influence of my parental upbringing and the remainder being my own personal life's experiences. Of course, I'm speaking as an adult away from parental care.

I had many unanswered questions about Bessie's life and her time in England during the war. I decided I would go to Canada again the next year but this time with Peter and for a longer period. Also, I hoped that I could persuade Bessie to come to England so that she could see me on my home ground. I wanted to show her where I grew up and for her to meet my family and friends. Like many adopted or fostered children, linking up with their mother after many years, the relationship was going to be unusual. Bessie hadn't watched me grow up. She had never dressed me, never disciplined me, nor seen me get married or have babies. It would be an adult relationship but one where never a cross word would be exchanged. How uncommon is that for a mother and daughter?

After my return from Canada, I needed to write a few letters. I stayed connected with Joan Barth from Parent Finders in Edmonton and Nancy Durham from CBC Canadian television. I wanted to keep them up to date with my news. They had been kind and helpful to me throughout my search for Bessie. I also needed to write to Brian White at the National Archives of Canada to tell him that I had been happily reunited with my birth mother. As might have been expected, I got no comment back from him. I do hope that he was secretly pleased that the reunion had gone well. Another letter was to Alice at the Royal Airforce Public Office at Kew. I received a lovely response from her saying that she was impressed with the story of my search and that she had decided to try and put in place a search scheme for similar RAF queries.

My next letter was to the Canadian High Commission in London enquiring whether I would be entitled to Canadian citizenship. Their reply was a bit surprising and upsetting. They told me that I could not obtain citizenship. They said I had automatically been a Canadian citizen up until my twenty-fifth birthday. As I hadn't renewed my citizenship in 1970, this meant that because I had allowed it to lapse, it could not be reinstated. That came as a shock, and I could hardly believe what I was being told. I had no idea that, at birth, I had automatically been a Canadian citizen. My obvious response was to ask how I could be held responsible for allowing my citizenship to lapse when I did not know that I was one of their citizens in the first place? My argument was dismissed, and the Canadian authorities were not interested in any appeal.

Over time, the weakness of the Canadian case meant that they eventually changed their rules. After a lot of enquiry and form filling, I was eventually granted full Canadian citizenship in 2019, backdated to my birth. It was symbolic in many ways, but naturally I was delighted and immensely proud. It seemed like justice had been done in that both my parents were in the RCAF, both were Canadian citizens, and I was born on Canadian soil at their Bramshott military base.

Chapter 25

Exactly a year later, in 1994, Peter and I flew to Vancouver for a three-week reunion with Bessie, Trish and Gail. We spent most of our time with Bessie. By now she had moved to a new apartment, close to the lively picturesque yachting area next to Granville Island, by the water at False Creek. It was an ideal place for Bessie; her new condominium featured the same arrangement and amenities as her previous place. When we were in Vancouver, we spent several nights with Daphne and Michael and some time in Nanaimo on Vancouver Island with Trish and Gail. It was a rerun of the previous year but this time much more relaxed. As we were in Canada for three weeks, Trish and Gail had organised that we should have a great holiday, seeing as much as we could of the local area. Part of the trip was taken up with travelling to Edmonton, Alberta, to meet the rest of the Hamilton family.

When we flew into Vancouver, Bessie, and her partner Les, met us at the airport. They were there at the arrivals gate, waving and smiling, greeting us like old friends who could not wait to see each other. Bessie had written about six letters to me over the previous year and we were settling into an easy relationship. Whether it was a 'normal' mother-daughter relationship, I'm not sure. She was not able to admit to her friends at her Billy Bishop Legion Club that I was her daughter. I was still a friend's daughter from London. I did not mind and played her game by keeping quiet about our real relationship. Being back in Vancouver was exciting ,especially as I had Peter with me. The downside was that Bridgette and James were not with us. But it was also good to see Trish and Gail again. I was beginning to get more information about the family history, especially about Bessie's siblings in Edmonton, where she had grown up.

Trish and her husband Randy had arranged a memorable trip driving eight hundred miles over the Rockies to Edmonton. Randy did the driving, with Peter, Bessie, and me in the back plus their two daughters Carrie, aged sixteen, and Leslie who was thirteen. Fortunately, Randy had a large eight-seater people carrier and there was plenty of room for us and the luggage.

The roads were straight and wide with little traffic. It was a stark contrast from driving on our busy motorways and narrow twisty country roads. Unlike the UK, there was no patchwork of roads connecting lots of small villages and towns. Any roads that left the main highway were tracks into the dense forest areas full of wildlife and bears. Away from the towns, small communities don't appear to pepper the countryside in British Columbia as they do in the UK.

If we had driven to Edmonton without stopping, it would have taken around twelve hours. We did not want to miss some of the beauty spots in the Rockies, though, so we took two days to get there and two days back home to Vancouver.

The first day, we drove just under four hours to Clearwater, near a town called Kamloops, where Marg, Bessie's wartime friend lived. We stayed overnight in a motel and spent time with Marg in her home.

Staying in the motel included an unusual event for Peter. When we entered the large room with an en-suite bathroom, there were two enormous beds. The beds seemed bigger than our king-sized bed at home. To our surprise, Bessie had decided that she would share a room with Peter and me. This was to keep the cost down by booking two rooms rather than three or four. Peter, having only met his mother-in-law for the first time a few days before, found himself sharing a bedroom with her. But Bessie was not at all fazed by the idea and it worked out fine. Peter and Bessie slept like logs – I was the one who stayed awake, worrying that my husband might start snoring, although it's fair to say that Peter does not often snore. I'm a light sleeper and don't tolerate snoring too well. If Peter does on the odd occasion snore, then a good shove with an elbow or a gentle tap on his head makes him turn off his back, which usually does the trick.

Bessie continued to remain fairly closed in relation to her emotions, which did not make it easy to question her about how she felt when I was adopted. However, between her and Marg, I learnt about their time in London during the war. When we went to Marg's house, she pulled out, from under her bed, an old fashioned brown rigid leather suitcase full of jumbled up photographs. Marg and Bessie rummaged through them till they found the relevant 1940s pictures. I was desperately wanting to ask if there was a picture of my father, but they were too occupied reminiscing about their time in London with the girls. I eventually took the plunge and asked Marg about him. She was able to produce one photograph which she was happy to hand over. It was a group picture of the RCAF crew in their flying suits in front of a Halifax bomber taken at their base at Linton on Ouse in Yorkshire. They said he was in 426 Squadron known as Thunderbird. During the conversation Bessie remained nonchalant, to the point of showing disinterest in my father. But over the years, following this visit, Bessie and Marg did drip feed me more snippets of information.

The chatter over the photographs brought out more details about how Bessie and Marg had first met at a place called Lachine, just west of Montreal. This was where military personnel were sent, for their final training and assembly, prior to going overseas for active duty. It was an RCAF station opened in 1941 as part of the British Commonwealth Air Training Plan. They were only there for a week to be given vaccines, rations, gas drills and their uniforms. The gas drill was designed more to test their nerve than it was to prepare them for an actual gas attack. They had to show that they could walk through a gas filled house, wearing a respirator, without panicking.

Their uniforms were "Air Force blue" copied from the British Air Force outfits with the jackets mirroring the men's having a belted waist. The skirts were "A" line, and the hats were a French "kepi" style with a peak. They were each given a shoulder bag made of artificial leather. The first thing that Bessie and Marg did was to take up the hem of their skirts. Under the "Instructions of Enlistment", this was not allowed! Bessie showed me photographs of when she was in London, off duty with her friends, looking decidedly wayward with ties askew, shirts hanging out, hats lopsided and hair out of control. However, there were also photographs showing the girls looking extremely professional in their RCAF regalia.

When Bessie and Marg enlisted, in 1943, thousands of Canadian women had signed up for the forces. About 1,300 Canadian airwomen ended up being posted to Britain. It was known that only the top recruits would be sent overseas, but in a non-combat support role. Bessie joined up partially for the excitement, to get away from home, to earn some money and, as she had told Daphne, to please her father. Bessie's father, my grandfather, had served as a soldier in the First World War. He and his brother were sent to the front line from their home in Ireland. Sadly, my great-uncle never made it home. He died in the trenches in France.

Before going to Lachine, Bessie told me that she went through a demanding programme of military training. She said that recruits were subjected to marching drills, learning the RCAF rules and regulations, etiquette and discipline coaching, occupational training, and physical education as well as flight training. Although they were part of Bomber Command, as women they were banned from combat flying. Their motto was "We Serve, that Men May Fly". By modern standards that seems seriously sexist. However, the Canadians redeemed themselves from that charge as in 1988, they trained the first women in the West to become fighter pilots. There were women flying in the Second World War in noncombat roles in Britain. These were female pilots in the ATA (Air Transport Auxiliary). They flew aircraft, alone without a navigator, from the factories to the front-line squadron bases.

Thirteen months after enlisting and following a brief period of home leave, Bessie and Marg left Canada aboard the Nieuw Amsterdam at Halifax, Nova Scotia, on 20 July 1944. After eight days at sea, they arrived at Gourock on the river Clyde in Scotland. Initially, their ship was built as a large Dutch cruise liner in the Netherlands and launched in1937. At the outbreak of the war, the liner was berthed in New York. When the Netherlands fell to Hitler's army, the Nieuw Amsterdam was requisitioned by the British Ministry of Transport as a Canadian troop carrier. Marg recalled that the boat was so large it could not dock at Gourock, and they had to transfer to smaller boats to get ashore. The journey across the Atlantic was the period when Bessie first met my birth father. He had assembled at Lachine and joined the Nieuw Amsterdam at the same time as Bessie.

Neither Bessie nor Marg said they felt nervous about the war they were about to join. They were too enthusiastic about their new venture to give any thought to the dangers that might lie ahead. The adventure of this new chapter in Bessie's life was exhilarating for an inexperienced girl from Edmonton. Being young, and in their early twenties, Bessie and Marg were looking to escape to a foreign land with all the fun of being away from home that it offered. When they landed at Gourock they crossed into England and were taken straight to a distribution centre in Cheltenham to be given their posting. The next event sounded a bit strange. The staff distributing the postings were difficult and offered a choice of either London or elsewhere. Bessie and Marg had been tipped off by those who had preceded them. They were told that new recruits would always be sent to the opposite place to the one they requested. Wanting to end up in London, Bessie and Marg asked for their posting to be "elsewhere" and at once got posted to London.

On the day they arrived in London, it happened to be one of the worst nights of the bombing by the German Luftwaffe. Bessie and Marg, along with other RCAF woman, were given short term temporary accommodation in an apartment in Kensington. When they heard bombs dropping, they said they had no idea what they were meant to do. They were terrified to such an extent that they cuddled up all night under the kitchen room table. Having been to the pub earlier where they drank beer, the inevitable happened, they needed to "spend a penny". The bathroom was halfway up the stairs, but they were too frightened to venture as far as the stairs. So, they took it in turns to "pee" in the kitchen sink. Bessie always claimed that after being in London her favourite drink was beer. After the flat in Kensington, they then spent some time at

Beaufort Gardens near Harrods before moving to their main place of residence at 11-16 Alexandra Mansions on the Kings Road, close to Sloane Square.

Both Bessie and Marg were sent to work in the basement of the famous Harrods department store in Knightsbridge. They used the side entrance to enter Harrods just off Hans Road. During the war, parts of Harrods transformed from selling luxury goods into making war time uniforms, parachutes, and aircraft parts. The basement was taken over by the RCAF logistics department. Given that the work was top secret, Bessie thought the management of the store was kept in the dark about the Canadians' task in their basement. Everyone was sworn to secrecy. Bessie and Marg's job was working in records, using cypher and code breaking systems. They recorded RCAF information such as postings, missions and those killed in action, which included aircraft that did not return home from bombing raids over Germany. Before leaving Canada for Britain, they had been given rigorous training on how to use these coding machines. The sensitivity of recording which bomber crew did not make it back from the German raids was an important part of their mission.

The first wave of severe German bombing was the blitz of 1940/1. By late 1944, there was a second wave of heavy bombing in London by the German V-1 bombs, the Doodlebugs or Buzz Bombs. The same bombs Bertha Rudow had heard when she was a nurse at Bramshott. This, of course, was a year before I was born. Bessie recalled how, one night, Harrods nearly took a direct hit from one of the V-1 missiles. It narrowly missed the main building, but the Harrods Estates Office took the strike along with the pub next door. Both were demolished. This happened in the early hours of one morning in August 1944. Bessie said this was the second time they were really frightened after seeing the damage that was done by the bomb. She came into work to find an enormous ugly black hole where the estate office should have been. However, they said generally when they were working in the basement in Harrods, they felt safe.

As Bessie and Marg recounted their wartime experiences, I got the impression that when rifling through the suitcase full of photographs, they were only recalling the good times and the comradeship they had had with the other Canadian girls. One of these was Mary, who I'd met when I first visited Bessie in her previous condominium. Young Canadian women, like Bessie, Marg and Mary, were away from home in a war zone feeling the need to make the most of their lives. Coping with the fear, uncertainty and distressing work, naturally made them seek out companionship and fun.

In the suitcase were many photographs of social events as well as the clubs that Bessie and Marg frequented. They mostly worked regular office hours, which left them free to socialise in the evenings and at weekends. Coming from Canada, they talked about how much they enjoyed skating and that one of their passions was watching their national sport of ice hockey. Most of the ice rinks in the war in London were closed. Trying to remember their ice-skating experiences, they thought, they took place in Richmond Ice Rink that had been kept open for the North American troops who regularly played ice hockey.

The Harrods Sports Club in Barnes was made available to the Canadians, but Bessie and Marg tended to go to the Roebuck pub near where they lived. The Roebuck was at 197 Kings Road and is now sadly closed. Dances were organised by the RCAF Overseas Headquarters. One dance that the girls went to was at Seymour Hall in Seymour Place just off Marylebone Road. This was a "Masquerade Dance" put on for the Canadians at two shillings and sixpence a ticket.

Bessie also mentioned going to Alexandra Palace for dances and roller skating. Alexandra Palace was certainly open some of the time during the war. Usually when they went out, they were in uniform. They coveted the designer clothes on the upper floors of Harrods but found them too expensive. Marg said when they got paid, they did treat themselves to lunch in the store. She told me she was the proud owner of a warm coat she had bought in London, although she admitted it was not from Harrods.

I asked about food, and they said in unison they hated the British sausages as they were ninety-nine per cent bread. They had ration books and shared whatever food they had, which in turn provided them with a reasonable diet. The ration allowances were like those of the US servicemen, which included food, cigarettes, stockings and chocolate. These were supplemented by parcels that came from the Legion clubs and families back home. Bessie and Marg mixed with other Canadians. They tried to get out of London whenever they had time off. Mary had an uncle who lived in York; hence they went north to see him and to meet the airmen from my birth father's Squadron. His 426 squadron also came south to London when on leave, which allowed Bessie to continue her liaison with my father.

Bessie had relatives in Northern Ireland where she was born. She visited them on occasions, sometimes taking Marg and Mary with her. They looked forward to leaving London, not because they feared the bombing, but because they liked travelling to see various parts of the country. Both Marg and Bessie commented that despite their first two encounters with the horror and devastation of the "V" bombs, they were not at all frightened and did not bother going to the shelters when the alert was sounded thereafter.

Chapter 26

After our stopover at Kamloops, Randy was keen to get on the road to continue our long journey to Edmonton. We had another five hundred miles to go. It was sad leaving Marg, as it was enthralling listening to all the wartime stories. I was grateful to her for pulling out that suitcase from under the bed and the kindness she showed towards me. The only detail I could not work out, was what happened when Bessie became pregnant. That was not touched on during the exchange of memories. Being realistic and thinking of one step at a time, there was likely to be a moment in the future to open that emotional door. I needed to hold back and bide my time. I was grateful to have been given the photograph of my birth father. When alone I studied this photograph trying to look at every minute detail of my father's face. Once I got home, I enlarged the photograph trying to make my father come to life. I tried to obtain some insight into his personality, which, of course, was ridiculous from only a photograph. All that happened was it made me want to know more about him.

When travelling towards Mount Robson, the highest peak in the Canadian Rockies, the scenery was spectacular. I felt fortunate to be driving this journey, with Trish and Bessie, on our way to meet my Canadian aunts, uncles and cousins. We passed through Jasper

National Park, famed for its world class skiing. We were close to a dramatic mountain range with a spectacular glacier plunging down the sheer face of the mountain called Edith Cavell. I was surprised and pleased to find the stunning Edith Cavell mountain in the Rockies, named after a British nurse. I had known about Edith Cavell during my nursing career, a person who was an inspiration with a true calling to help all those who suffered. She worked in occupied Belgium in 1915 and was executed by a German firing squad in Brussels at the age of forty-nine. She was an exceptionally dedicated person whose only 'crime' was helping the injured on both sides of the conflict.

We arrived in Edmonton late in the day. The welcome Peter and I got at my Aunt Jean and Uncle Jim's house was exceptionally warm. Jean was Bessie's youngest sister, being the baby of the family at the age of sixty. Currently, Bessie was seventy-two and I was forty-nine. Bessie, Peter and I stayed with my Aunt Jean for three nights. Trish, Randy and the girls went to be with one of their cousins.

Like most houses in Canada and especially in Edmonton, they have enormous semi-underground basements, which are like complete apartments with bedrooms, a bathroom and lounge areas. The extremes of temperature between summer and winter are stark in Edmonton. This means that the foundations of the house, including the water pipes, are sunk eight feet down, being well below the frost line. The purpose of the deep foundations was to stop the house footings moving during the freeze and thaw cycle. This created the space for a basement which is frost-free in winter and cool in summer.

When my grandparents first arrived from Ireland in the late 1920s, they ran a farm in the countryside near Edmonton. It must have been a shock for them when they encountered their first winter. It's understandable that they eventually quit farming and took up work in the city with more comradeship and warmth.

On arrival at my aunt's house we found that a family barbecue was organised for the next day, so that all the cousins, aunts and uncles could meet Peter and me. I was not prepared for the enormity of the family welcome. I hadn't met anything quite like this when growing up in England. We were a compact family who did not often get together for group celebrations apart from weddings or funerals. The Hamilton family were vastly different. Every few years they would organise a family reunion. They took it in turns to host the event. It was usually during the summer holidays to allow as many as possible to attend. A venue would be hired, an itinerary organised, invitations sent out, and an enormous celebration cake would be bought from Costco. As the family were originally from Ireland, the bunting theme would be green shamrocks, and everyone would get a souvenir mug plus other goodies all with the same Irish green theme.

I had arrived amid a family who were clearly close. They all knew each other intimately and were there to help with each other's problems. I was intrigued by this Hamilton family to whom I now belonged. Most of the relatives in Edmonton turned out for the barbecue in Aunt Jean's garden, or yard as they called it. There must have been thirty of us. One of the attractions, I'm sure, was that they wanted to see what Bessie's oldest daughter looked like. I had to rely on Trish to give me the family details and to keep reminding me of everyone's names. It was a sincere welcome and we sat late into the evening chatting round a large outside fire pit. The next day we went sightseeing in Edmonton and we visited my grandparents' grave.

It was then time to set off on the long journey back to Vancouver, which proved just as enjoyable as the journey out. We took a different route home, going through Calgary and Banff, spending the night at Radium Hot Springs. Our scenic tour of the

Rockies continued with a quick stop to see Lake Louise. The next stop was Lake Peyto. We parked the car in a forest area and walked a short distance on a path between the pines to a viewing point. The place was deserted, and I was not sure what we were going to see. What a wonderful spectacular emerged, it was a perfect spot to look down on this idyllic deep turquoise green lake with its colour coming from glacial silt. The Peyto glacier was creeping down the mountainous valley feeding into the head of the lake.

It was glorious driving through the Rockies going for miles and miles without seeing another car, just moose and elks along the roadside. The long hours of travel allowed me to get a comprehensive history of the Hamilton family from Trish and Bessie. I was then able to make sense of the family tree. We stayed the night in Vancouver before catching the morning ferry to Vancouver Island to link up with Gail. Bruce and Gail hadn't made the journey to Edmonton as they were both working.

From Bessie's condominium in Vancouver, we could see Burrard Bridge with all the yachts in False Creek as well as looking towards Granville market. One building seen from her balcony was the famous Molson's brewery. In Canada, they would call Molson's a beer, but of course Peter, being an English real ale enthusiast, would refer to it as lager. It was a favourite drink of Bessie's and was one of the drinks sold by the jug at the Billy Bishop Legion club. A feature of the brewery building was a tall clock tower. Whenever we wanted to know the time, we would look at the tower and refer to it as Molson time, which happened also to be a euphemism for 'time for a beer at the Billy Bishop'.

On Vancouver Island, we spent time with Gail and her family, swimming in a fantastic hidden cove and finding sand dollars on Rathtrevor Beach. Sand dollars are a flat type of sea urchin about the size of my palm and looking like a large coin, hence the name.

Another day we took a trip to Long Beach and Tofino on the west side of the island. Peter wanted to say he had swum in the Pacific, so he took a dip in what turned out to be freezing water just like the North Sea. Nobody else was swimming and he did not stay in long. I realised how fortunate I was to be meeting my birth family who lived a third of the way round the world in such a beautiful place. The city of Victoria, in the south of the Island, was a place we had to see. It's the capital of British Columbia, a beautiful coastal city with a flavour of English elegance and architecture.

I was sad that our time to return home was approaching. We made time to spend a few days with Daphne and Michael in West Vancouver. We visited Peter's uncle Ivan and caught up with my friend Sylvia. Daphne and Michael took us to Squamish about thirty miles north, which was halfway up Highway 99 on the way to Whistler, the well-known ski resort. The town of Squamish has a big logging industry, with huge collections of logs in the water that were floated downstream to the sawmills for processing. An impressive landmark dominating one side of the town is The Chief, a gigantic granite rock face that towers over Squamish. It has a sheer ascent for seven hundred metres and is a great draw for fearless climbers. On scanning the cliff face, we could just make out the dot of at least one climber, part way up.

We caught the flight home on Sunday 14 August having been away for twenty-three days. The holiday had been one of the most astonishing journeys of my life. Meeting many of my birth family and seeing the country that was their home, left a huge impression on me. There were many gratifying memories. Most people get to know their relatives over the period of their early years. I had met mine all in one astonishing go. On this visit I felt truly integrated into the family. My next goal was to try and coax Bessie and my sisters to come to England and see my home.

Chapter 27

The following year in 1995, Bessie made the trip to England to stay with us in Wakefield. On the day she arrived, we happened to be going to a wedding at Lumley Castle, near Chester-le-Street in County Durham. My planning for Bessie's arrival hadn't worked out well. The wedding was the daughter of a close friend from when we had lived in York. We did not want to miss her wedding. Bessie seemed happy enough to go ahead with the wedding plan and she was duly invited to come with us. Fortunately, she was a relaxed, easy outgoing sort of person. She did enjoy herself, but she must have been tired after the long-haul flight. We were staying in the castle, and I had booked Bessie a quiet room away from the evening celebrations.

When I was seventeen, I used to go to the odd party at Lumley Castle. At that time, it was one of Durham University's halls of residence. Having grown up in Durham City and living in the Cathedral precinct, I wanted to show Bessie my old home. The day after the wedding we drove to the town of Durham. I was able to take her to the Cathedral, where Peter and I were married. Also, she could see the house where I grew up. We walked along the attractive riverbanks and saw the old prison, close to the centre of the town, where Peter began his Prison Service career.

My brother lived in Durham. I thought I would introduce him to Bessie. However, that turned out to be a problem. Bessie was keen to meet him and my convivial sister-in-law. My brother was adopted like me, but three years before I was born. He had issues with being adopted, to the point that he found he could not emotionally accept coming face to face with my new-found mother. We are all different and I respected his choice not to meet my birth mother. Whereas I viewed the circumstances of war differently and accepted that liaisons were ignited during fraught times of conflict. My brother was disturbed by the notion that his mother had given him up at birth. He could have explored his birth heritage, but he deliberately chose not to; this shaped his attitude towards my own search. He did not want to hear about it or have any kind of contact with my new family. In his eyes they did not exist. He thought I was being disloyal to my adopted parents and to him.

During the early part of Bessie's stay with us, she met my friends. We travelled to London, and she reminisced about Harrods and showed me where she used to live. We walked along the side of Harrods, down Hans Road to find the door she used to enter when going to work. She described the euphoria of the VE Day celebrations on 8 May 1945, after the Germans had unconditionally surrendered to the British and Western Allied Forces. Bessie must have been five months pregnant at that point but that did not stop her joining in the singing and dancing in Trafalgar Square.

While Bessie was in England, I took her to meet my colleagues at Huddersfield University. The staff treated her like royalty, in turn she charmed them with her scintillating smile. I also wanted to take her further north in England to see Northumberland. When we went to Bamburgh, on the Northumberland coast, we made the decision to economise by borrowing a friend's trailer-tent. It seemed an excellent idea at the time, and it all worked out well.

Although, I can't suppose Bessie had been camping before in her life. Looking back now, I don't know what I was thinking. But at seventy-three, she took it in her stride. It was only for a couple of nights and, luckily, the weather was good. We pitched the trailer-tent alongside my ex-nursing friend Sheila's caravan in Bamburgh. Fortunately, we could retreat into the caravan to a comfortable seating area and have our meals with Sheila and her husband.

While we were in Northumberland, we visited beaches, many castles, and Holy Island. Little did I know then that Peter and I would move to Northumberland and that I would work for the National Trust as the manager of Lindisfarne Castle and Seaton Delaval Hall. By the time we left Northumberland, we thought amusingly, that Bessie must be completely "castled out".

Bessie loved playing cards, which was something in common with my Durham mother. Along with the spoons, which were in her handbag, she always carried two packs of cards. A particular card game she liked, we called "Bessie's game". It was something she might have invented. It was a cross between Whist and Rummy, but there were no partners, and two packs of cards were used. It was great fun as well as being highly competitive.

One of the places that we took Bessie to stay was the Kirkstile Inn, in Cumbria, close to the cottage in the Lake District where we regularly stayed as a family. It was a convenient place to visit as it was on our way to Stranraer where we would catch the ferry to Northern Ireland to visit more of Bessie's family.

In the evening, we had the small comfortable hotel lounge to ourselves, where of course we played cards and had a few drinks. Late in the evening a young couple came in from the bar and asked if they could join us and play Pontoon. Peter and I were quickly out of the game which left Bessie playing on. The couple then suggested they should play for money but not high stakes. They looked at

Bessie presuming that they could take this old lady for "a ride". They might have thought they could make a little money to pay for their drinks. By now it was getting towards midnight, but Bessie was up for the challenge. Card games were her thing, and she was exceptionally good at them.

More drinks were ordered, and the game continued. Bessie was in her element and on a winning streak. The more the couple lost their money, the more they drank, the more alert Bessie became. After an hour, Bessie's winnings accumulated to about twenty pounds. The couple eventually gave up and went to bed looking disgruntled. It was brilliant watching my mother take them to the cleaners. What a laugh we had. However, it was probable that the hotel would never have allowed the gambling if they had known what was going on. But an elderly lady sitting up late, had to be harmless.

The next day we boarded the ferry to cross the Irish Sea to stay with a cousin at Randalstown in Northern Ireland. There was more family to meet on my grandmother's side. They were kind and generous in the way they welcomed us. We visited the family grave at the tiny, picturesque church at Duneane. I had never been to Ireland before, so touring around was fascinating, especially seeing the Giant's Causeway. Since then, I have been several times to visit the family I first met with Bessie. As Bessie was born before the official division of the South from the North of Ireland, she found it hard to understand the "Troubles". She was only six when she left Ireland. Thanks to Bessie's roots, I have recently managed to get a full Irish passport along with citizenship. Because of my two mothers and the legacy they left me, I'm proud to have British, Canadian and Irish citizenships.

The visit to Northern Ireland was an important one for both Bessie and me. There was a wide family circle that relished having renewed contact with Bessie. Her mother, my grandmother, had been a branch of the Bruce clan, marrying a Hamilton, and then emigrating to Canada. The older ones were pleased to see Bessie return. I got the same reception as when I had been welcomed into the family in Vancouver and Edmonton.

In the period before our visit to Northern Ireland it would have been foolhardy for somebody like Peter, as a prison governor, to go there. In the past, the hostility between the Loyalists and the Republications had caused much fighting and many deaths in and around Belfast. By the time we went in 1995, though, we thought it was regarded as relatively safe for people in a government security role to visit.

One evening we went out for a family pub meal in Randalstown, there were about twelve of us. As the evening wore on, one of the group asked Peter what his job was. Previously he would have mumbled something about being a civil servant. Now with matters being more settled, he said openly, he was a prison governor. But Peter's remark was overheard by others around the table and the atmosphere suddenly became tense. There were worried looks to see if people on other tables close by might have heard. A remark like this to have been picked up by an IRA (Irish Republican Army) supporter, might have spelt trouble. One of my cousins told me never to let Peter say what his job was while he was in Northern Ireland. We were surprised that the tensions around the whole of the Loyalist and Republican conflict were still simmering. We left Northern Ireland after five days with some lovely memories and it was a journey that Bessie had particularly enjoyed.

During another time when Bessie flew over to stay with us in England, she became famous for playing her spoons. Peter, at the time, played the banjo with a New Orleans jazz band, called the Tweed River Jazz Band. I took Bessie to hear the band play, which of course she loved. Naturally, in her handbag was her set of spoons. The leader of the band, who played the trumpet, invited her to join them for a couple of numbers. She was happily in her element, rhythmically and professionally running the spoons across her knees and up her arms in time to the music. On later visits to England, Bessie repeated the performance, and the band leader, Peter Roughead, took quite a shine to this lively Canadian spoons' virtuoso.

My third visit to stay with Bessie in Vancouver was in August 1996. One of the family reunions was happening and being organised by Trish and Gail on Vancouver Island. Of course, I had to be there. This time Peter did not come with me, but my friend Vivienne came. It was the first time she had been to Vancouver and was keen to meet all my family. Vivienne had been on my journey during the search for Bessie. She was with me when CBC did the filming at Alderbrook Park. The family reunion took place in a hall at Lantzville, just north of Nanaimo. It was loads of fun, with aunts, uncles and cousins arriving from Alberta and British Columbia. There were forty of us there. Trish and Gail had laid on a large barbecue. It was an excellent party but a lot of hard work for my sisters. I still have my Hamilton mug, sporting a shamrock, which was in our "goodie" bag to take home.

Another evening, we went to the Billy Bishop Legion Club, as per usual, for a drink. Bessie was in her third year as President. Over the years I got to know several of her legion friends. Bessie had still been describing me as the daughter of her friend from the war in England. On this occasion, though, unexpectedly without forewarning, Bessie stood up in the busy bar and announced that she would like everyone to meet her daughter. People paused for a moment with some murmuring that they already knew Bessie's two daughters and thinking the drink had taken hold. "No," said Bessie, "what you don't know is that I have three daughters. This is Catherine, the baby I had in London during the war." There was a marked silence in the room, then suddenly everyone wanted to come over and chat to me. They welcomed me to their Legion club, as if I had been part of the war effort.

Vivienne thought I had known about the announcement in advance, but no, it was a complete surprise. I was in shock. The Canadian clubs have a strong affiliation with Legion clubs in Britain, so embracing a long-lost child from the war was significant to them. It was an extraordinary experience, catching me offguard but in a gratifying way. With all the chat going on, I was not given time to dwell on the enormity of what Bessie had just said. It must have taken great courage for her to make that announcement. At last, my birth was out in the open and this was an enormous milestone for me in my quest to be completely accepted by my birth mother. After so many years of deception, it would have taken a monumental leap for Bessie to build up to that simple declaration. Any stranger in the bar would certainly have wondered what on earth was going on.

In the Billy Bishop, that same evening, was a new member who had just emigrated from Newcastle upon Tyne to live close to her daughter in Vancouver. She was fascinated by our story and sat for an hour or so, talking to me and Bessie. This lovely Geordie woman, unknowingly, took on the role of prompt, which got Bessie to open up about what had happened to her during the war. I will call this Geordie woman Anne. Sometimes it's helpful to talk through another person to be able to voice what we really feel about each other. Anne asked all the questions that I was too inhibited or too polite to ask. I listened while Bessie answered her questions in an honest and open manner. I sat like a bystander and took it all in. Bessie and I are two people who control our emotions and sometimes mask how we are feeling. To have Anne there innocently drawing out of Bessie how she felt about her wartime pregnancy was quite amazing. It was as if she had been planted to act as the catalyst between us.

It would have been hard for Bessie during those first five months in London when she concealed her pregnancy from most of her colleagues. She was aware that if knowledge of her pregnancy had been known, she would have been sent back home, by boat, to Canada before the five-month gestation period was up. After that point, it was considered unsafe for a pregnant woman to travel by boat across the Atlantic during wartime. The only people who knew were her closest friends. She was adamant that she would give birth in England and that no one in Canada should learn of my existence. She was too ashamed to face her family. Also, she was determined not to have an abortion because she felt she had to give birth to this baby. In early pregnancy, abortions were offered to many wartime single mothers, especially those in the forces.

Prior to this, I had learnt from Marg that Bessie's heart was broken when she went back to Canada and left me behind. Marg said Bessie often looked at blonde-haired blue-eyed girls in the street and wondered what I would be like. Bessie talked to Anne about how, after her convalescence following my delivery, she returned to Alexander Mansions in London and was relieved to see all her friends still there, especially Marg and Mary. Marg did not leave until May 1946, just a few months before Bessie returned to Canada. Back home in Canada, Marg and Mary kept Bessie's secret, that is until the day Trish asked her friend Elaine, Marg's daughter, about me. In fairness to Marg, the fact that this question was asked made her think that the subject was out in the open.

There was also the question of my birth father. Bessie accepted that after she became pregnant their relationship had ended and that he had fallen in love with an English woman in London. Although he knew about the pregnancy, she never put any pressure on him, and she decided to take full responsibility for their actions. Giving birth to me was something she had to sort out on her own. Neither Bessie nor I, have ever held a grudge against the man who fathered me. Times were strange during the war. However, the barriers and stigmas towards having a baby out of wedlock were prevalent during this period and for many years to come.

I have since traced my birth father's family. I never met my birth father, which is a sadness that was out of my control as he died of cancer as a relatively young man just before his fifty-ninth birthday. He and his English wife lived in Ontario with their four children. I have met the family and my half-siblings. I fully understood how difficult it was for them to accept me as their father's daughter. But I'm extremely grateful to have met them all and to have them welcome me as part of their family. When visiting Vancouver, I will occasionally fly into Toronto to meet up with them and stay for a few days with my three half-brothers and sister.

Epilogue

I might have had a disadvantaged start to my life, but I regard myself as being privileged to have two mothers of whom I can say I loved, yet in quite diverse ways. Although my Durham mother died in 1983, in my eyes I'm still the little girl who she cared for, gave me a family home, a grounding in life and encouragement to pursue whatever path I wanted to take. Bessie turned into the mother who I respected and liked enormously, and I have grown to relish the fact that this person was the one who gave birth to me. However, I have to say it was strange when almost fifty years old, I bonded with a stranger who was my mother.

What I have learnt is that there is no rule book as to how a mother and daughter should approach each other after such a long absence. The past can't be undone, and I'm comfortable with that. What counts is how I embrace the future and find a fulfilling and comfortable way to move forward. Now the subject of "who am I?" does not enter my head and it's not something I need to dwell on anymore. My Durham sister-in-law came up with a quote, "never view history through the prism of today". I'm not sure where the quote comes from, but it certainly reinforces how I feel about not judging my birth parents' behaviour during the Second World War. And leaving me behind in a foreign country.

Bessie helped to fill in all the missing gaps I perceived about myself, and I'm now comfortable with my identity. I have recovered from feeling disloyal to my Durham mother. In a way, it's like coming to terms with allowing my voice to say that I still have three children, not just two after Stuart died. The agony of Stuart's death is forever in the core of my being. The slightest trigger makes me feel so sad for what might have been. It's a sadness that will never heal. One mother knew Stuart but never experienced the pain of his death. The other mother never met Stuart but knew he had died. And as a mother myself, I carry the grief of the death of my eldest child.

The grief is a powerful overwhelming emotion that affects every part of my being and has changed my life for ever. Subconsciously I wanted to hand over my suffering to Bessie and for her to share my pain. But of course, that could not happen as Bessie never met Stuart. She showed empathy and kindness but not deep understanding. I needed my Durham mother to do that but that could not happen.

I'm content embracing both my adopted family background and my birth family inheritance, and I cherish both families. Maybe I'm just lucky to have had both, to have the genes from one mother and nurture from another. Such a wonderful journey of discovery only happened because I was adopted, and I would not have changed it for anything.

Over the years, I have visited Canada many times and Bessie came to England on numerous occasions. Trish and Randy continue to come and stay with us every few years and we have taken trips into Europe with them. Peter and I once had a superb holiday after flying into San Francisco from Australia, to meet up with Trish, Randy, Gail, and Bruce. Over four days we drove up the US west coast, through the Californian vineyards, up into Oregon and Washington then eventually across to Vancouver Island.

I went to see Bessie just before she died in March 2013, aged ninety-one. We both knew it would be the last time we would see each other. It was hard walking away and coming back to England. We had managed to connect as mother and daughter. In fact, towards the end of her life she forgot that I hadn't always been with her from birth.

I miss both my mothers dreadfully. Violins and spoons sum them up well, so dissimilar but with a common link. Perhaps the link was music, or it was me. What is missing in this story is how my Durham mother felt about not being able to conceive her own children and the emotions around adopting me. She took her innermost feelings to the grave. I'm sad about that and often chastise myself for not asking her more about her life at the time of my adoption.

I feel fortunate to have had both my Durham mother and Bessie in my life. I'm grateful for the sacrifices they, in their separate ways, made for me. My Durham mother's legacy is all around me, in the area where I live, in the material things that I have inherited, and most of all my character and personality gained from my upbringing. Bessie gave me another perspective and provided me with the genetic makeup of who I am.

Now, thirty years after first meeting Bessie, I have no qualms about discussing my heritage. I carry no shame relating to my birth. I'm proud to have my three citizenships and happy to explain how they came about. I feel the same excitement from all those years ago in school when I first found out that I was adopted before the teacher dampened my enthusiasm.

My sadness is that I can't share the discovery of Bessie with my Durham mother and my son, Stuart. However, I regard myself as fortunate to have had two mothers. And that Bridgette and James knew them both.

Maybe my birth parents were not the right people to bring me up. And my Durham parents made the best job of giving me a stable happy home. However, I do conclude and believe that it should not have taken almost fifty years before I knew anything about my birth family.

Recently, Peter and I commissioned a bench, organised by the National Trust, in memory of Stuart at the side of Crummock Water in the Lake District. It was his favourite spot. On a brass plaque, on the leg of the bench, it simply says his name, date of birth and date of death and a reference to Dire Straits' "So Far Away". Neither of my mothers will ever sit on Stuart's bench. However, for the rest of the family it's a place to go and remember.

An elderly friend once said to me, "You are privileged, you have two sets of parents and their respective families. Most of us don't have that option." How true is that.

I have fulfilled what I set out to do. I found my birth mother. I gave her back her daughter with the bonus of grandchildren and great-grandchildren. I had broken the chain of the unhappiness of three mothers. I did it for myself but also for my children, Bridgette and James. The cycle of tragedy had been broken for Bridgette when I made connection with Bessie. Violins and Spoons are instruments of emotional expression, they create melodic sounds and rhythmic vibrations, that link two women who never knew each other.